Fra

Loire Valley

Jarrold Publishing

CONTENTS

Chinon

This is the Loire Valley

There are a number of reasons why the Loire, rather than the Rhône or the Seine, should be considered as *the* river of France, even though it does not flow through Paris. It is longer than the other two and it flows through the heart of France, far away from any borders, thus being known as the country's main artery.

The Loire does form a border in a subtle way, but visitors will not find it easy to detect differences between the two sides of the river. Anyone who comes from the Ile de France or its nerve centre, Paris, however, does not really begin to relax until reaching the banks of the Loire, for the people here are calmer and more friendly than those living in the north. Life is simpler and more pleasant, the climate milder and the vegetation more abundant. To the observant tourist it will become apparent that south of the Loire the towns are smaller and the streets not quite so crowded. The pace of life there is much slower, and the people appear to have much more time to spare.

The course of the Loire is more varied than is generally supposed. From its source in a farmyard 1408 m high in the Massif Central the river flows southwards, but it soon makes an about-turn to the north and then for a long stretch runs almost parallel to the Rhône/Saône rivers, which have taken the direct route south towards the Mediterranean.

Millions of years ago, during the Tertiary period in the earth's history, the Loire flowed further northwards and at some point joinèd the River Seine. But later as it encountered new barriers of rock it swung more towards the west, where by that time

The Loire at St-Benoît (HTM-CRTL)

the sea had already encroached as far as the region of Blois. Gradually however the sea retreated and the river with its tributaries followed. Now the Loire turns off in a westerly direction near Briare, reaches its most northerly point close to Orléans and does not take a general east-west course until just beyond Blois.

The Loire, to those not familiar with it, appears to be a mighty, almost untameable river. It has extreme variations in water level: 116 cm in March and 18 cm in August have been recorded at the bridge of Briare. Heavy Atlantic rainfall combined with the thaw in the Massif Central leads to regular flooding, sometimes catastrophically, as in 1846 and 1966. The towns which stand on the river bank still bear the high-water marks. Embankments were constructed in particularly vulnerable areas, but it was soon realised that the fast-moving mass of water merely broke the banks of the river elsewhere and flooded unprotected areas along the river margins.

With modern technology it should be possible to dam the river completely, but the current of a river 'controlled' in such a way would only be accelerated. The old bridges would eventually no longer be able to withstand the powerful pressure of the water, especially in the winter, when ice-floes weighing many tons can be hurled against their piers — a frightening sight indeed.

In the meantime great catastrophes have been avoided by the overflow basins which have been constructed along the river. The flood water is able to flow away more slowly from them, and from time to time the fertile silt left behind is distributed over the land. There are now ten such basins between Nevers and Tours. In addition dams have been built in the upper reaches of the river to attempt to control it.

In the Loire Valley

The Loire presents the onlooker with two quite different faces. In the spring it is a mighty and wild river which tears up everything in its path and floods the meadows far away from its banks. In the height of summer, however, it appears to be a modest water course, meandering around sandbanks and islands which are carpeted with lush pasture grazed by cows; it even looks as if it could be crossed on foot.

In spite of all the difficulties, human enterprise has succeeded in making the Loire into a useful waterway. In the Middle Ages it served mainly as a transport route for bulk goods, including the building materials for castles and cathedrals. For the return journey the flat, wide barges were loaded with wine, provisions and other goods and then towed upstream. When the wind was in the west a sail made it easier for the men on the towpath to pull the barge upriver. With the increased mobility of the population and the development of a road system capable of carrying stage coaches, the Loire actually grew in importance as a highway. Orléans became the 'Quay of Paris' and Madame de Sévigné had her coach floated down the river on a Loire-raft on her journey to Nantes. She asserted that she had 'never seen anything to compare with the beauty of this route'.

When the first steamships left Orléans — they were named *Les Inexplosibles* to reassure the passengers — a new era seemed to have begun in river traffic. Yet steam power, which was to have boosted the river's importance, in the end only destroyed it. The railway was faster and more reliable. The last river steamer was taken out of service towards the end of the last century, and only fishing boats were left to glide silently over the river and its tributaries once more.

Essential details in brief

The Loire: 1012 km long, it has its source 1408 m up in the volcanic cone of the Gerbier-de-Jonc in the south-eastern region of the Massif Central. There are great variations in water level and the river, which is the longest in France and drains one fifth of the country's surface area, is navigable from Angers. It discharges its waters into the Atlantic close to St-Nazaire at an average of 800 cubic metres per second.

The Valley of the Loire: The section of the river between Gien and Angers, taking in the most important tributaries.

The most important tributaries: Cher (with the Sauldre), Indre, Vienne, Maine (with the Loir).

Châteaux: Over 300 well-known ones, about 100 of which are open to the public.

The Garden of France: The description reflecting the fertility of the region with its abundance of vines, fruit, vegetables and flowers.

Population: Approx. 1.5 million.

Largest towns: Orléans (pop. 110,000), Tours (pop. 145,000), Angers (pop. 143,000), Nantes (pop. 263,000).

Regions: Nivernais, Orléanais, Blésois, Touraine, Anjou.

Most famous châteaux: Amboise, Azay-le-Rideau, Blois, Chambord, Chenonceau, Chinon, Cheverny, Villandry.

Dreamy Loire landscape

The Valley of the Loire

It is difficult to define the Loire Valley clearly, either geographically, historically or culturally. The term is not used for the Massif Central, for example, where the upper reaches of the river have cut most deeply into the earth's surface. But it is extensively used where it is quite inappropriate, because of the difficulty in identifying the actual floor and sides of the valley. Even when the kings of the House of Valois lived here, however, the *Val de la Loire* was a much used term, especially in literature. This is perhaps best explained by the need for scenery of such beauty to have a description which is pleasing to the ear as well. The 'Valley of the Loire' has a much more attractive ring to it than simply the name of the river itself.

There seems to be general agreement that the Loire Valley actually signifies the area on both sides of the river beginning roughly between Sancerre and Gien and ending downstream from Angers, including the tributaries within this region, chiefly the Cher, Indre, Vienne, Loir and Maine — in other words, the 'land of the royal châteaux'. It is remarkable that administrative boundaries play no role at all in defining the region. It is divided up into about a dozen *départements* but the historic names still persist. Nobody pays particular attention to whether he is in Loir-et-Cher, Indre-et-Loire or Maine-et-Loire, whereas the regions of Orléanais, Touraine and Anjou have very specific associations.

The Garden of France

It is not difficult to describe the scenic charm of the Loire Valley. The Garden of France, a description reflecting the fertility of the region, is the most common metaphor, although this is not the only enthusiastic term used in brochures to describe the area. The novelist Honoré de Balzac described Touraine, where he came from, as a 'potential paradise'. The Garden of France is not wholly the result of nature, however. Many industrious 'gardeners' have been at work here for hundreds of years in order to make the land as productive and flourishing as it is today.

Those who have been to other regions in the country will soon realise when they come to the Loire Valley that the soil here is used intensively; it is the most cultivated and productive region in France. Yet there are still vast areas of moorland and heath, tracts of land lying fallow, and wooded areas.

Delicious sheep's milk cheeses and aromatic forest honey are produced in modest quantities. The habitat of small game is a closely guarded secret shared only by enthusiasts. Some of the high plateaux which lie behind the river banks are, however, surprisingly barren, providing a fascinating contrast to the Garden of France which should not be missed.

The predominant picture is of a prosperous region with a mild, equable climate, coupled with a fertile soil which is enriched by silt deposits. Narcissi, lilies and hydrangeas grow untended by the sides of the roads. There are lush fragrant lilacs, pale violet wisteria hanging like beads from the walls of the houses and beautiful shrubs and hedges in the gardens. The finest chestnut blossom anywhere can be seen in the château grounds of Sully, Chaumont and Chenonceau in May, when the blooms

Cycling in the Loire countryside

in the high treetops are at their best.

The Garden of France is not an ornamental garden, however, but mainly a kitchen garden. In spite of increasing industrialisation, the people of the Loire Valley make a living predominantly from general agriculture. Wine production (see page 19) plays a major part; high-grade vegetables (asparagus, artichokes and beans) and fruit (apples, pears, greengages and cherries) are in great demand in Paris and usually bring in an excellent profit. The farmers in the region thus do very well. But on the other hand they have a long, hard working day, especially in the summer. Visitors who speak French should take any opportunity to talk with them. They are outgoing, not without a sense of humour and very easy to understand as the most cultured 'High French' in the country has long been spoken here.

The good life

The high plateaux, less fertile than the floors of the river valleys, are largely given over to arable and stock farming. Huge fields of corn and maize can be seen, as well as pasture land on which white Charolais cattle graze with large flocks of sheep. The villages in the Loire Valley cannot be called picturesque and often appear to be somewhat dull and featureless. But if you keep your eyes open as you drive through the countryside, particularly in Touraine, you will often see large stately farmhouses surrounded by shady chestnut trees, beeches or elms. There is almost always a large orchard close by, and often a chapel, a bakehouse and a duck-pond.

The traditional vinegrowers' houses, with their tiny windows, the oven built into the wall, and the external staircase above the entrance to the cellar, are unfortunately rarely seen nowadays. On the other hand, 'cave dwellings' hewn out of the soft, volcanic rock of the river valleys, which are to be found in the region around Vouvray in the Loir valley and on both sides of Saumur, are greatly sought after by families fleeing from city life. The finest old farmhouses and water-mills no longer belong to farmers or millers, but in all probability to lawyers or architects from Paris who wanted to fulfil their dreams, by no means cheap ones, of leading a simple but stylish life in the country.

Wine-growing

French kings from the 14th to the 17th centuries

House of Valois

1364–1380	Charles V
1380–1422	Charles VI
1422–1461	Charles VII
1461–1483	Louis XI
1483–1498	Charles VIII

Charles VIII

House of Valois-Orléans

1498–1515	Louis XII

House of Valois-Angoulême

1515–1547	François I
1547–1559	Henri II
1559–1560	François II
1560–1574	Charles IX
1574–1589	Henri III

François I

House of Bourbon

1589–1610	Henri IV
1610–1643	Louis XIII
1643–1715	Louis XIV

Louis XIV

🔖 Phases of History

The chronicled history of the Loire Valley begins at the time of the Gallic War (58–51 B.C.) when Julius Caesar conquered Gaul. At that time, the Roman general was particularly involved with the Carnutes who were established between Orléans and Chartres and who were resisting against Roman domination. The tribal names of the Turones (people from the district of Tours) and the Andecavi (from the district of Angers) have also been passed down to us through the records left by Caesar. After Gallic resistance had been finally broken, Gallo-Celtic culture and Roman civilisation very swiftly merged. The Gallo-Roman period played a far greater part in shaping French history than did the later era of Franco-German rule.

Christianity began to gain a foothold in Gaul about A.D. 250. The first known missionary was St Gatien, Bishop of Tours, to whom the cathedral there is dedicated. St Martin of Tours (316/7–397), Roman soldier turned monk, was eventually elected Bishop of Tours in 371 because of the miracles attributed to him. Through his deeply religious beliefs, righteousness and unremitting readiness for action he exerted a great deal of influence in Gaul. Following his death he became the favourite saint and patron of the Frankish Empire; 500 towns bear his name and he remains the patron saint of the poor. He is buried in the Basilica of St-Martin in Tours where countless pilgrims assemble each year on November 11th.

The Merovingians and Carolingians

The vacuum which was created by the fall of the Roman Empire was filled by the Franks who had been advancing westwards from the Rhineland. At the end of the 5th c. their king, Clovis, occupied the region to the north of the Loire and in the year 498 was baptised a Christian in the cathedral at Rheims. His successors, the infamous Merovingians, extended Frankish rule to the country south of the Loire. The decline of the Merovingian dynasty in the following two centuries was accompanied by the rise of a governing body of court officials, whose most senior representative was known as the *Major Domus* ('Mayor of the Palace'). The family of Pepinids or Carolingians succeeded in installing themselves in this office on a hereditary basis, and were thus the actual rulers. In A.D. 732 one of them, Charles Martel, engaged the Saracens who were advancing northwards at that time, and defeated them in a fierce battle between Tours and Poitiers; as a result the only Saracens to reach the Loire did so as prisoners. In 751 his son Pepin became the sole ruler of the Franks after deposing the last of the Merovingians. Charlemagne (A.D. 742–814) was Pepin's son and although he took up permanent residence in Aachen, Orléans remained the undisputed capital of the West Franks. The monasteries of St-Benoît-sur-Loire and St-Martin-de-Tours developed into cultural centres the fame and influence of which spread throughout the Christian west.

It was not until the Norse invasions in the second half of the 9th c. that the Loire's heyday came to an end. The Vikings, who came up the great rivers in their longboats, plundered the land so thoroughly that hardly any of the Loire's buildings from the early Christian period have been preserved. The last Carolingian king was so weak that he permitted his regional vassals to set themselves up as feudal lords, which is why small, virtually sovereign states were established around Blois, Tours and Angers.

The rise of the French monarchy

The counts and barons were constantly at war with one another. Since great progress had been made in the art of warfare by that time, they erected castles on almost every hill in their territories and from these strongholds they were able to attack and to defend themselves against their enemies.

Foulques Nerra, Count of Anjou, who lived around the year 1000, was one such lord who rose through the feudal system. His enthusiasm for building castles can be seen in the number of (now ruined) *donjons* or keeps. Although it is not always immediately evident, many of the Loire châteaux stand on the foundations of these early fortresses.

Hugues Capet was elected king of France in the year 987, and thus began the long and difficult rise of the French monarchy. It was another hundred years before Louis VI was able to start bringing the insubordinate vassals under the control of the Crown. But then his successor quite unwittingly put everything at risk. Louis VII divorced his vivacious wife, Eleanor of Aquitaine, who immediately married Henry Plantagenet, Count of Anjou. The count had scarcely had time to rejoice over the considerable dowry, which included south-western France, when he succeeded to the throne of England in 1154. A confrontation very soon developed between Henry II of England, who now ruled more than half of France, and the king of France, to whom little more than a third of his country remained. Since Angers was the central issue in this dispute, there followed constant invasions, sieges and conquests in the region of the Loire.

Philippe Auguste, an extraordinarily clever and indulgent ruler, worked for over 30 years of his long reign to drive out the English, step by step. He was helped in this by family feuds in the House of Plantagenet involving Richard the Lionheart, and fortune favoured France from then on. Louis IX, later St Louis, defeated Henry III of England and under the Treaty of Paris in 1259 regained most of the French territory which had been lost. The kingdom was thus consolidated and strengthened.

The Hundred Years War

The Hundred Years War between England and France (1338–1453) was brought about by the death of the last French king of the Capetian line, when King Edward III of England laid claim to the throne of France. The English, who were the more advanced in terms of battle techniques, first occupied the south-western part of France and then the whole of the north. From time to time hostilities would cease and there would be a truce, sometimes even for years. Then circumstances would change and fighting would break out again.

When in 1418 Paris fell into the hands of the duke of Burgundy who had ties with England, and the under-age successor to the French throne, the Dauphin, later Charles VII, had to leave the city under cover of darkness, all seemed lost. The region of the Loire now became the last refuge of the Dauphin who was mockingly called the 'King of Bourges' by his opponents, but he was even driven out of that city, and the English laid siege to Orléans. Then the great unforeseen miracle occurred.

Joan of Arc (c. 1412–1431) emerged as a saviour on the scene of French history. The shepherdess from Lorraine, so the story goes, heard voices calling her to assist the king of France. She at once set out for Chinon (see page 65) where she found the Dauphin, and despite his hesitation persuaded him to place her in charge of a small

Château d'Ussé
Joan of Arc statue, Orléans

army. After liberating Orléans, she went on to defeat the English in two further battles. With the assistance of Joan of Arc the Dauphin was crowned in Rheims, which finally confirmed the legitimacy of his royal status. Wherever she went Joan of Arc awoke the new nationalistic feelings of the French people. Following a fruitless attack on Paris, however, she was captured by the Burgundians at Compiègne and sold to the English for a large sum. Charles VII abandoned her and made no effort to help her in any way. Taken to Rouen by the English, who now kept cleverly in the background, she was brought before the ecclesiastical authorities charged with witchcraft and heresy. She was burned at the stake in the market place of Rouen on May 30th 1431.

Joan of Arc had performed a miracle — the restoration of the French monarchy to France. As a result a previously unknown feeling of national pride swept through the country. Admittedly it was decades before the English were completely driven out of France, but when Charles VII died in 1461, he left behind a France that was free and to a great extent united.

The Royal Loire

It may seem a coincidence that the liberation of France had its origins in the Loire region, in Orléans and Chinon, the only territory which still remained in the hands of the 'King of Bourges'. Yet it is certainly no coincidence that for almost 200 years France was governed from this area, and that its cultural development was shaped from here. At that time Paris was considered ungovernable. The kings of France found in the Loire region, on the other hand, everything which seemed to them useful and beneficial: security, central position, residences, freedom of movement, prosperity and quality of life.

The history of France during this period is the history of its kings: their good deeds and their outrages, their marriages and divorces, their followers and their adversaries, who were at least people of rank if not princes of the royal line. The common people played no part in this. They toiled, suffered and lived under conditions about which we know little, as nobody considered them worth recording. The French Revolution was a long way off.

Charles VII ultimately earned himself a good reputation despite his weak beginning. He bequeathed to his son and successor, Louis XI, a relatively well filled treasury and a regular army of considerable fighting power. Louis XI knew how to put both to good use. He avoided wars whenever possible, but he used the army as a means of exerting pressure, and he was not mean when it came to buying men or ideas. Although the monarch, who preferred to live in his modest château at Plessis-lès-Tours, was a bigoted fanatic and oppressor, he left behind an unparalleled list of achievements at the end of his long reign (1461–83). He had eliminated his most dangerous opponent, Duke Charles the Bold of Burgundy, in 1477 and brought Artois, Maine, Anjou and Provence under the power of the Crown, together with Roussillon and Franche-Comté. By doing so he gave France its historical borders which in the main are still in force today, and set it on the road to becoming a great power.

Charles VIII, the son of Louis XI, therefore had a secure inheritance. 'No other kingdom in Europe was at that time so widespread, so populated, so united, so rich.' (Michel Mollat.) Yet the young king was not content simply to enjoy this state of affairs. Following the regency of his aunt, Anne de Beaujeu, he wanted to accomplish great things — greater even than his father had done. He set his sights on Italy, where France could lay a dubious claim to the kingdom of Naples. In 1494 he made his first march across the Alps, without of course realising that he was initiating, on Italian soil, the struggle between the great powers for supremacy in Europe.

The Renaissance in France

Charles and his successor, Louis XII, as well as François I, were drawn towards Italy again and again. France had only just left the Middle Ages behind and it was felt that the way forward lay in Italy, which stood for all the cultural values associated with the Renaissance — art, humanist literature and learning, progress and civilised living. So a strange picture was emerging. On the one hand, the French kings were at war in Italy, allied with or fighting against the Habsburgs, Venice, Rome, England, Aragon, Switzerland and the Italian princes. They were celebrating victories or suffering defeats, being taken prisoner (as was François I), signing peace treaties and then dishonouring them, and finally setting in train the conflict between France and the House of Habsburg which, in the following centuries, became the main problem in Europe. On the other hand, each time they went to Italy, the French kings brought back with them anything which would enhance life in France, that is to say, in the Loire Valley above all. It was not just new ideas and styles which were brought back, but also the people who had created them: master-builders, artists, decorators, landscape architects, tailors, cooks, and one Leonardo da Vinci, who spent the last years of his life in Amboise as artistic adviser to François I. There was even a poultry farmer who introduced the first incubator into France.

François I (1515–47) more than anyone embodied the new consciousness and optimism of the Renaissance. The opposite of the miserly, bigoted and misanthropic Louis XI, he was considered by his contemporaries the personification of the knightly virtues. He was courageous, strong and enterprising. He loved women, luxury and hunting, but also the fine and noble arts, as is demonstrated by the châteaux at Blois and Chambord where he continued building as soon as he returned from his Italian campaigns. The portrait by Jean Clouet suggests he was not particularly good-looking, but his successes with women were legendary. He was less successful in politics. He lived off the capital accrued by his predecessors and demanded of his country enormous sacrifices in both blood and money. Yet the French forgave him.

Henri II (1547–59) ruled just long enough to enable him to withdraw gracefully from the Italian adventures of his three predecessors. Yet the conflict between the House of Habsburg and France remained — on two fronts, for the king discovered that he could throw the Holy Roman Empire into great insecurity if he played off the German princes against the emperor, and he made every effort to prevent an agreement between them.

France had greater problems with Spain, which under Philip II, the son of Emperor Charles V, was pushing ahead to become a leading power in Europe. It was hoped that a 'political' marriage might reduce hostility between the two states and an alliance was arranged between Philip II and one of Henri II's daughters. The highlight of the wedding celebrations in Paris was a grand tournament, during which however the French king was mortally wounded. The forty-year-old king left a politically inexperienced widow, Catherine de Médicis, and three under-age sons, in whose hands lay the fate of France for the next thirty years.

Gloomy Times

François II married Mary Stuart but 'reigned' for only one year (1559–60). Although only ten years old, Charles IX succeeded him and survived until 1574 when Henri III (1574–89) became king. He did not like women and consequently remained without an heir. He was murdered by a fanatical monk a year after his mother died.

It was once again a time of confusion and gloom. The rousing festivals of Amboise and Chambord had been forgotten. The Reformation had swept through Switzerland and was heading towards France. On the Loire and in the west of France the Calvinists, known in France as Huguenots, had a particularly strong following. The Catholics were led by the dukes of Guise and the Huguenots by the Bourbons, the Prince of Condé and Admiral Coligny. Both parties fought with every means at their disposal for influence and power in the royal court. The Catholics were supported by Spain and the Huguenots by England. Catherine de Médicis tried to intervene but could not prevent the two sides from constantly being in conflict.

The Religious or Huguenot Wars (1562–98) were a succession of warlike excursions interspersed with periods of exhaustion. There was destruction, pillaging, assassination, murder, intrigue and treachery. The bloodiest moments, after the macabre prelude at Amboise in 1560 (see page 74), were the St Bartholomew's Day Massacre in Paris on August 24th 1572, when about 3000 Huguenots out of about 20,000 in the entire country were put to death, and the murder of the duke of Guise in Blois in 1588 (see page 59). For this murder Henri III had to pay with his own life. He had, however, taken precautions prior to his death and had paved the way for Henri de Navarre of the House of Bourbon to become his successor. The latter ascended the throne as Henri IV and within a few years was able to bring about a settlement between the two warring parties, thus bringing the Religious Wars to an end. The Edict of Nantes (1598) guaranteed the Huguenots freedom of conscience throughout the country. Some years previously Henri had become a Catholic, and by so doing opened for himself the gates of Paris, a city which had previously been hostile to him (*'Paris vaut bien une messe'* — 'Paris is well worth a mass' — was his comment). From then on France was ruled from Paris, or from Versailles, with only a few interruptions. The Loire Valley's 'royal period' became a nostalgic dream.

Castles and Châteaux on the Loire

There are few regions in the world where châteaux and fortresses are so densely concentrated as in the area between Orléans and Angers. The Loire Valley is certainly the only region where they follow each other in such close chronological order. The castle and château buildings are like a picture book whose pages can be turned to disclose a history of stylistic development. A record can be found for almost every decade from the 10th to the 18th centuries, although there are few details of the period when castles were first built. The earliest remains are usually considered to be the foundations of the rectangular *donjon* or keep in the park of Langeais, which dates from the year 990. The outer walls of later donjons from the 11th and 12th centuries still stand, for example those in Beaugency, Montbazon, Montrichard and Loches. Reconstructions give us an idea of the primitive conditions in which even the ruling families of that time had to live.

Gradually the donjon was replaced by the castle; this comprised a massive circular wall reinforced with watch-towers and surrounding an inner courtyard in which there

Angers

were other buildings. Examples are in Angers and Chinon, and the largest one from this period is in Loches, where an entire town was enclosed within the castle walls. The 'picture book' castle with its moat, battlement walks, pitch holes and drawbridges developed from this in the late Middle Ages. Examples can be seen at Sully-sur-Loire, Chaumont, Langeais and Ussé.

During the 15th century attempts were made to improve the accommodation inside the castle walls and to make living more comfortable. Rooms and windows were larger and the monotony of the façades was broken by decorative work. Particular attention was given to roofs, on which ornate chimneys and dormer windows were built. The lower parts of castles, on the other hand, remained austere in appearance as they were still required for defence purposes when the need arose. The castle in Saumur is typical of this phase.

With the Renaissance the defence function was completely abandoned. The castle became a palace, a residence for the king who thought less of governing the country than of enjoyment and ostentatious living. Amboise, Blois (François I's wing) and Chambord show this development. Even the nobility and the financiers who had become wealthy in the king's service built their own stately homes, the finest of which may be seen in Beauregard, Chenonceau and Azay-le-Rideau. Towards the end of the 16th century the court moved to Paris and the Loire Valley became a provincial

Château de Saumur

region, but it still retained its great attraction. Aristocrats with sufficient resources built country seats in the classical style. Those at Cheverny and Ménars are the best known.

There are over 300 châteaux along the banks of the Loire and its tributaries, and 100 of them are open to the public. Some good advice which has always applied to eating in France but which is just as relevant when it comes to sightseeing is: do not take on too much! Nobody, not even the most enthusiastic, could cope with twenty castles during the course of a week and at the same time derive enjoyment and benefit from them. It would perhaps be possible under perfect conditions, but the inevitable guided tours give visitors little chance to pick out the things which are of most interest to them.

Food and Drink

Experienced visitors to France prefer to have just one good meal a day which is usually taken in the evening after a day's sightseeing. Lunch is often limited to a sandwich or a snack. In towns and cities these may be purchased ready prepared from many bars and are usually accompanied by a beer, a glass of wine, or a cup of coffee. In the country the alternative could be a picnic in the open air, but if you plan to do this you must make sure you get everything you need in good time, as most shops close at midday for lunch. As there is fresh bread again in the afternoons, *flute* or *baguette* loaves are often sold out before midday. A small piece of pie or cheese, fresh fruit, a light rosé wine or a mineral water would go well with the bread.

When you arrive at your hotel you may be asked if you will be dining there. If you have not already discovered the most popular eating-place in the vicinity, however, you should do so. You will certainly not be disappointed, as the majority of little local restaurants offer meals which are extremely good value.

The pleasure derived from food increases immeasurably if you are able to cope with the linguistic demands of the menu. The terminology used in French cuisine is so varied, however, that even those with a good knowledge of the language sometimes have difficulty. But do not hesitate to ask. The waiter will take the trouble to explain to you what is available. Anyone interested in such an important matter as the composition of a menu or the recipe for a certain dish will be treated with respect.

Specialities

Despite the 'royal' past which the Loire and its tributaries can boast, the traditional cuisine of Orléanais, Touraine and Anjou is rather plain and simple. As an hors-d'oeuvre, *rillons* and *rillettes* (potted shredded pork made with fat extracted from crackling) are particularly popular, as are the solid *andouillettes* (sausages) made with chitterlings, pork and bacon. Although the water in the Loire is no longer quite as pure as it might have been at one time, up to now it has not damaged the health nor impaired the flavour of the fish caught here. *Brochet* (pike), *carpe* (carp), *alose* (shad) and *sandre* (pike-perch) are all caught in the river and are served in white butter (*beurre blanc*) or in white wine (*marinière*), or baked (*rôti*).

Chicken traditionally takes precedence over other meat. It is seldom frozen and until a few days before reaching the table the birds have probably been running around the farmyard. There are, of course, many other ways of serving chicken besides *coq au vin* (chicken in wine sauce). You will often find on the menu *carré de porc* (breast of pork), *gigot de mouton* (leg of lamb), and *gibier* (game), the latter coming predominantly from the Sologne. Vegetables and fruit are plentiful in the Garden of France.

There is usually a large selection of cheeses on offer in French restaurants. The small grey-skinned cheeses made from goat's milk (*chèvre*) are typical of the Loire region. The best known of these cheeses are the *crottins de Chavignol*.

Wines of the Loire

The careful pruning of vines is supposed to have originated in the Loire district. During St Martin's time donkeys from the monastery of Marmoutier, close to Tours,

Enjoying a drink in the open air

are said to have broken out of their enclosures and made their way through the vineyards, trampling over leaves and eating young vines as they went. The horrified monks were quite surprised to find that the vines which had been eaten did not die but bore the finest of grapes in the following year. Ever since then vines have been pruned.

'Loire wines do not travel well' used to be the explanation for why these wines were not well known outside France, but today they are available in many countries. The white Sauvignon wines of Sancerre and Pouilly, especially the smooth *Pouilly Fumé* with its light flinty taste, have become highly regarded over the past few years. Red wine from Sancerre is also good to drink but is only available in that region.

Another large area extending along both sides of the Loire above Tours produces white *Pinot*. *Vouvray* is a dry or semi-dry light sparkling wine which matures in cellars within the limestone rocks. It is extremely pleasant and its best vintages can be quite sweet. *Montlouis* from the left bank of the Loire is often processed as a sparkling wine, as is *Saumur* from further downstream. The best red Loire wines come from around *Chinon* and *Bourgueil*. They also mature in rock cellars before acquiring their ruby-red colour and when opened they give off a highly prized fruity aroma. They are pressed from cabernet grapes which grow in Bordelais, and are at their best when chilled to a temperature of 16–17°C. *Rosé d'Anjou*, the wine which is most widely produced and which can be obtained from almost every supermarket, does not require such precise treatment. Good and very good white wines, such as *Coteaux du Layon*, are also produced in Anjou. The very best wines come from the region of *Savennières* and *Château de Serrant* and include *La Coulée de Serrant* and *La Roche aux Moines*.

Hints for your holiday

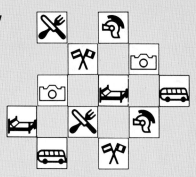

In the land of the royal châteaux

There is no ideal route through the land of the royal châteaux. In the next part of this book you will find suggested routes which can help you to plan your holiday, but if the ideas for the various detours do not appeal to you, then you can make your own itinerary. However, do not feel you would be wasting time by taking such detours. Your progress will probably be just a little slower than you had worked out on the map at home, but if you accept that and drive so that you can enjoy the scenery those detours could turn into the most memorable you have ever made.

The most important and renowned châteaux in the region are described in detail on pages 56–90. If you choose those which appeal to you most you can plan your route accordingly. A lot can be left to chance, but it is probably best to bear in mind the motto: 'As much planning as necessary — as much freedom as possible'. Perhaps the best idea is to choose say five châteaux to visit without fail, and to take in as many others as time and opportunity permit.

Where to go and what to see

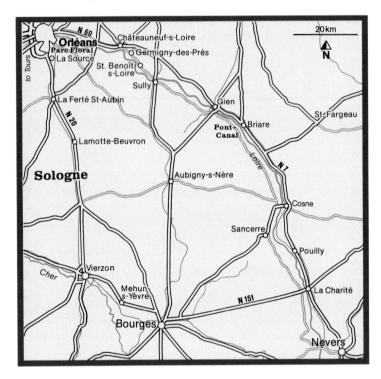

From Nevers to Orléans

The region of the Loire and its tributaries has been made more accessible by good scenic roads, so it really does not matter whether you bear right or left when you reach a fork, provided that you keep the main direction in mind. Those who follow the general rule of avoiding major roads will profit most. This rule probably holds good everywhere but particularly in France, as even minor country roads are well maintained and well signposted, yet relatively little used.

Nevers Alt. 186 m. Pop. 46,000
This rather sleepy provincial town, after which the Nivernais region is named, is situated at the point where navigation began on the Loire. Stones and wood were shipped from here to the great castle-building areas on the river, as were the very fine items of earthenware pottery or faience which have made Nevers famous among connoisseurs.

Just five minutes from the Place Carnot where there is a large car park you come to the *Place Ducale* in the historic centre of the town. Here stand the former *Palais Ducal*, a 16th c. Renaissance building, and the *cathedral* which was built between the 11th c. (crypt and apse) and the 16th c. Close by, at 16 Rue St-Genest, is the *Musée Municipal* which contains a notable collection of faience pottery. Further eastwards you come to the splendid Romanesque *Church of St-Etienne*, built in the second half of the 11th c.

If you are in a hurry you can take the N7 to Sancerre going via La Charité, where the lovely old bridge and the 11th–12th c. *Basilica of Notre Dame* are worth seeing, and the wine town of Pouilly where the excellent *Pouilly Fumé* white wine is produced. It is, however, more interesting and more pleasant to drive along the left bank of the river beside the canal.

Sancerre Alt. 312 m. Pop. 2,300

Sancerre is a picturesque little wine-producing town on a hill overlooking the Loire. Because of its exposed position, it was often fought over during the Hundred Years War and the Huguenot Wars. All that remains of the fortress is the 15th c. *Tour des Fiefs*; the former keep is now a bell-tower and may be climbed on Sundays. There are picturesque old alleyways with shops selling Sancerre wines as well as *crottin*, the goat's milk cheese which is a speciality of the town. Panoramic views over the vineyards and the countryside along the banks of the Loire may be enjoyed from the *Promenade Porte César*.

 Hotels and restaurants: *Rempart, Rempart des Dames*.

 Bourges

Bourges may be reached in just under an hour from Nevers, La Charité or Sancerre. The town, which has a population of 80,000, would hardly be worth a visit were it not for the presence

Bourges

of one of the great Gothic cathedrals of France which is considered equal to those of Paris and Chartres. The *Cathedral of St-Etienne* was built between 1195 and 1260; the doorways on the west front and the stained glass in the choir chapels are particularly fine.

The route continues from Bourges along the Loire canal, the idyllic charm of which is only seldom disturbed by a boat. Close to Briare the canal crosses the river via an aqueduct, the *Pont du Canal*, which was a technical sensation in the year 1894. The maritime emblems moulded from cast iron proclaim the pride of the new iron age. A little further on Gien appears on the right bank of the Loire.

Gien Alt. 161 m. Pop. 16,000

The skyline along the river bank is clearly dominated by the *château* and the *church*, both of which were so badly damaged during the last war that they had to be largely rebuilt. There is a *hunting museum* in the château which houses numerous trophies and also a large collection of works by François Desportes, who was artist to the court of King Louis XIV and famous in his day for his paintings of dogs.

A special tip

Button-collectors will be in their element in the *Musée International de la Chasse* (hunting museum). At the time of Louis XIV, it was fashionable for huntsmen to wear garments with elaborately decorated buttons. Numerous fine examples depicting deer, dogs, wild boar and other appropriate motifs may be seen on display in the little museum.

Sully Alt. 119 m. Pop. 6000

(For information on the château see page 68.)

 Hotel: *Esplanade*, with views of the château.

 Restaurant: *Hostellerie Grand Sully*.

 Mid-June to mid-July: summer concerts.

The Abbey Church of St-Benoît-sur-Loire

Seven kilometres further on after crossing the bridge to the other side of the river, you come to the abbey church of St-Benoît-sur-Loire, one of the finest and most famous Romanesque buildings in France. The abbey was founded in the 7th c. under the name of Fleury, and about the year 675 one of the abbots succeeded in having the remains of St Benedict, the founder of the order, brought from the devastated monastery of Monte Cassino to the abbey on the Loire, which gained enormous prestige as a result. The monastery flourished particularly at the time of Charlemagne and his son Louis the Pious. Every science known about at that time was taught in the monastery school, which became a centre of learning in France, and fine illuminated

Capital, St-Benoît-sur-Loire

manuscripts were produced in the scriptorium.

Following the Norse invasions, when the abbey suffered badly, a new golden age began around the year 1000, with the monastery taking the lead in a far-ranging reform movement. The foundation of many new monasteries was initiated from here and, in the following two centuries, the abbey church was built. The monastery itself was destroyed during the Napoleonic period and it was not until 1944 that a new community of Benedictine monks was established in St-Benoît.

A massive two-storeyed *porch* dating from the early 11th c. and built to a square ground-plan forms the front of the church. The pillars with their half-columns make an impressive forest of stone with fascinating sculpted decoration. Fifty-four capitals on the ground floor and seventy-eight on the upper storey have motifs ranging from the acanthus leaf to animal and hunting scenes, as well as scenes from the life of Christ and representations of the saints and the Apocalypse. However long you look you will always be able to discover something new. The 17th c. top section of the tower is unfortunately totally inappropriate.

The triple-aisled *nave* is early Gothic (1150–1215). The *transept* was completed at the beginning of the 12th c. as was the choir, which is a particularly splendid example of Romanesque architecture. The doorway on the north side still bears some original 13th c. column figures and there are some beautiful choir stalls of 1413 at the crossing.

In the *crypt*, which dates from the second half of the 11th c., the vault radiates from a massive central pillar which contains the tomb and relics of St Benedict.

Germigny-des-Prés is 6 km beyond St-Benoît-sur-Loire. Here there is a small chapel which was built about the year 800 as a kind of annexe to St-Benoît. Little remains of the original architecture. The chapel is famous for its Byzantine mosaic which was created by an artist of the Ravenna School. It consists of 130,000 coloured tiles and represents two large archangels pointing towards the Old Testament Ark of the Covenant which is watched over by cherubims. The hand of God is thrust down from heaven and appears through the clouds. The mosaic, of a type unique in France, dates from the period between 820 and 850, and was restored during the last century. A lovely 13th c. statue of Mary, carved from limewood, stands in the chapel.

It is a further 30 km to Orléans from Germigny-des-Prés via Châteauneuf-sur-Loire and the N60.

Orléans Alt. 110 m. Pop. 110,000

Quite frankly, to the unprepared visitor the town tends to be something of a disappointment. It is not only a traffic junction and a commercial centre (wines, foodstuffs and textiles), but it also suffered repeated devastation in the Hundred Years War, the Huguenot Wars and finally the Second World War. Thus despite the historical importance of Orléans the local colour of the old town, its atmosphere, and the appeal of its artistic monuments have inevitably been somewhat diminished.

The most important event in the town's history was the siege by the English in 1428–9 and its liberation by Joan of Arc in May 1429. Its return to the French on May 8th, when the English abandoned the siege and Joan entered Orléans in triumph, is celebrated annually in the town with an extensive programme of festivities.

As long ago as 1344 the duchy of Orléans was created in order to make provision for the younger sons of the royal line. Consequently, the ruling king very often found himself opposed or even conspired against by the inevitably jealous duke of Orléans.

📷 **Place du Martroi.** This is the centre of the town with the *Statue of Joan of Arc* (1855). The Rue de la République leads from the square to the station and the Rue Royale to the Loire which is bridged by the lovely *Pont Georges V* (c. 1760). The Rue d'Escures, where you can see houses once owned by 16th c. noblemen, runs eastwards to the Place de l'Etape. The *Hôtel de Ville*, the Renaissance town hall built about 1550, is on the western side of the square. In the garden in front of the building is a statue of Joan of Arc at prayer.

Cathedral of Ste-Croix. Although very large this is not one of the 'great cathedrals' of France. Over the centuries it has been constantly added to, enlarged, renewed and repaired (13th–20th c.). The only artistic masterpieces are the early 18th c. wood carvings in the choir, based on designs by Mansart, Lebrun and Gabriel.

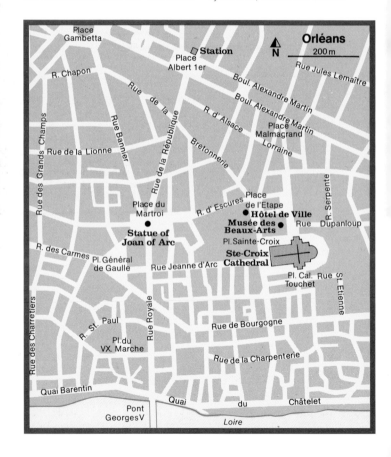

Ste-Croix Cathedral, Orléans

Musée des Beaux-Arts. The Museum of Fine Arts with its notable collection of paintings by French artists lies to the north of the cathedral complex. It is housed in the old town hall. A *town tower*, built in the 15th c., can still be seen in the courtyard.

La Source, a suburb south of the Loire, lies about 10 km from the town centre. The *Parc Floral*, an attractively laid out botanical garden close to the modern university, is best known for a natural curiosity. The supposed source of the Loiret, a tributary of the Loire which 'rises' here, is nothing more than a branch of the Loire which reappears here after flowing for a stretch underground. There are many peaceful romantic places on the banks of the Loiret, with old country houses and mills which are either in ruins or have been converted into weekend accommodation.

🛏 Hotel: *Escale du Port Arthur*, St-Hilaire/St-Mesmin on the banks of the Loiret.

🍴 Restaurants in Orléans: *La Crémaillère*, 34 rue Notre-Dame-

Orléans

de-Recouvrance; *L'Assiette* near the Place du Martroi.

 May 7th–8th: Joan of Arc festival with the presentation of colours, bands, military parade, torchlight procession and festive illuminations.

🚌 The Sologne

The region which lies to the south of Orléans between the Loire and Cher rivers is known as the Sologne. There are comparatively few places of cultural interest here. The Sologne, which stretches for miles, is flat and thinly populated. Woods, meadows and moorland alternate, and although not popular with water-sports enthusiasts the many lakes attract anglers and nature-lovers to their shores. The Sologne is, however, strictly speaking under cultivation: under Napoleon III the marshes were drained, canals were cut and woods of mainly Scots pine and birch were planted — very much as in the Landes of south-west France. Since that time agriculture has flourished even here, including stock farming and the cultivation of fruit and vegetables (asparagus, strawberries, etc.). However, the main products of the region are those which are as yet outside the range of 'organised' agriculture: partridges and pheasants, hares, ducks, berries, honey and mushrooms.

There are plenty of alternative routes for those who intend to take a detour through the Sologne, but try to avoid travelling across it on the N20 from Orléans to Vierzon, as this road becomes very crowded. You would be best advised to consult a road map and choose the roads which most appeal to you. The smaller the roads, the more they are to be recommended. You could combine a trip through the Sologne with a visit to the châteaux of Cheverny (see page 70) and Chambord (see page 56) which in a sense form the western border of the region. On the drive there you could follow the course of the Loire, and on the way back you could take the road from Blois to Sancerre.

🍴 Restaurants: in the Hotel *Lion d'Or*, Romorantin-Lanthenay, 69 rue Clemenceau; *Croix Blanche*, Chaumont-sur-Tharonne.

From Orléans to Blois

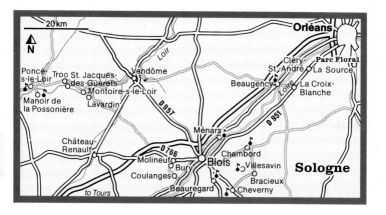

This stretch takes about half an hour on the *Aquitaine* motorway. If you use the N152, however, you must allow longer and the journey will not be very enjoyable owing to the numerous lorries which use this road. The recommended route is thus along the left bank of the Loire on the D951, which leads you out from the suburbs of Orléans into a less densely populated and more scenic region.

Cléry-St-André Alt. 96 m. Pop. 2100

The *basilica* stands at the entrance to the town. The church tower dates from the 14th c. and the church itself was built in the 15th c. on the foundations of an old pilgrimage church. The interior is plain and rather austere. Louis XI is buried here with his wife, Charlotte of Savoy. A magnificent monument with a statue to this unpopular king was completed in 1622; it stands to the left in front of the Lady Altar. The tomb in which the remains of the royal couple are buried is close by. The Renaissance *Chapel of St James* in the south aisle is decorated with the emblems of pilgrims on their way to Santiago de Compostela. The *choir stalls* are lavishly carved and the magnificent doorway in the sacristy is in the Flamboyant style.

On leaving the basilica, make for La Croix-Blanche 'crossroads where you turn right towards Beaugency.

Beaugency Alt. 106 m. Pop. 7300

This little medieval town, strategically positioned on an important crossing point on the Loire, was once heavily fortified. It was held by various feudal lords and was often fiercely fought over. All that remains of the old castle is the huge 11th c. keep, an impressive tower even though only the outer walls have survived. Housed in the château which was built in the early 15th c. by Count Dunois, Joan of Arc's companion in arms, is a regional museum, *Musée des Arts et Traditions de l'Orléanais*, with displays of furniture, costumes and rural crafts.

Opposite the château stands the *Abbey Church of Notre-Dame*, which dates from the 12th c. although this is

Château de Villesavin

not obvious. Not far from here there is a small square with a *Memorial to Joan of Arc* and the *St-Firmin Tower*, a remnant of a 16th c. church. The Rue du Change which leads into town will take you to the *Hôtel de Ville* (town hall), a splendid Renaissance building, and to the *Tour de l'Horloge* (clock tower) which originally formed part of the town's defences.

Above the Loire in the south of the town there is a lovely view of the river from the tree-lined terrace of *Petit Mail*. A walk along the river bank is very enjoyable.

❌ Restaurant: *L'Abbaye* in the monastery ruins opposite the bridge.

Back on the left bank of the Loire, the D951 passes a nuclear power station and then continues along the embankment for 15 km on the last stretch of the journey to Blois. The wide river with its islets and sandbanks is always in view. To the south of the road lies the vast Forêt de Boulogne with the Parc de Chambord, and if you wish to take in two of the large Loire châteaux in this area you will have to head away from the river.

(Château de Chambord: see page 56.)
(Château de Cheverny: see page 70.)

On the drive between these two châteaux you pass through the holiday resort of Bracieux. There is a somewhat smaller stately home nearby which is not often visited, the Château de Villesavin.

The Château de Villesavin is a charming Renaissance building. The present owners have gone to great lengths to preserve the threatened structure of their home. Of particular note are the dormer windows and the inscriptions on the rear façade, the tastefully furnished rooms, the kitchen with its original fittings, a beautifully sculpted *Renaissance fountain* and one of the few 16th c. *dovecots* to have survived the French Revolution. The majority were destroyed as they were looked upon as symbols of aristocratic extravagance.

On the road from Cheverny to Blois you pass the entrance to the Château de Beauregard which, like Villesavin, is one of the less visited though lovely Loire châteaux.

(Château de Beauregard: see page 88.)

Blois Alt. 73 m. Pop. 52,000

(Château de Blois: see page 59.)

Even at the time of Charlemagne, the counts of Blois were a powerful aristocratic family. In the following centuries they were forever extending their influence and possessions — as well as the fortified castle which secured both — until they were no longer able to prevent their property from falling into

the powerful hands of royalty. Châtillon, the last count of Blois, was forced to sell his estates to Louis of Orléans, the brother of Charles VI, in order to pay off his debts.

During the 15th and 16th c. the stretch of the Loire between Orléans and Tours was in effect the centre of France. Among the various residences which the Crown occupied at that time, Blois was by far the most important, and unofficially looked upon as the capital of France.

Today Blois is a bustling, friendly provincial town. You can stroll along streets which have a pronounced medieval character and also through modern pedestrian precincts with all kinds of attractive shops. Like Tours, Blois is classed as one of the most important tourist centres of the region.

From the *Place Victor Hugo,* a good starting-point, you can get to

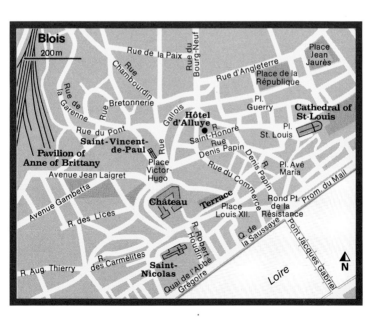

Blois

the terrace on the western side of the château. In earlier times it formed part of the castle garden which Gaston d'Orléans extended as far as the site on which the railway station stands today. From the terrace there is an interesting view of two of the façades of the château, the *François I Wing* (Renaissance) and the *Gaston d'Orléans Wing* (classical), and looking north-west you can also see the *Pavilion of Anne of Brittany* which, like the terrace, once formed part of the castle garden (about 1500). Today it is the *Office de Tourisme*. The former Jesuit church of *St-Vincent-de-Paul* (17th c.) stands to the right of the pavilion.

To the east, the towers of the *Cathedral of St-Louis* are the dominant feature of the town. The church, which was destroyed by a hurricane in the 17th c., was rebuilt in the Gothic style but will not appeal to many visitors, although the route there is worth taking. In the Rue St-Honoré you should visit the *Hôtel d'Alluye*, a stately Renaissance palace built in 1508 by a financier. The inner courtyard with its Italian arcade and the

spiral stone staircase with palm vaulting are both worth seeing. Quiet, steep old alleys lead from the cathedral back to the Rue Denis Papin and into the pedestrian precinct.

Between the château and the Loire, towering over the surrounding houses, stands the most magnificent church in Blois, *St-Nicolas*, in which Romanesque and Gothic stylistic elements are happily united (12th–13th c.). The capitals in the Romanesque choir are splendid.

 Restaurant: *La Péniche*, Promenade du Mail.

 Excursions

Forêt de Blois
A delightful stretch of woodland known as the Forêt de Blois adjoins the western part of the town. You can drive through the forest on the D766. In Molineuf, an old mill town, you come to the valley of the Cisse. The neighbouring villages of Bury and Coulanges are also worth a brief visit. Dotted around here and there are picturesque ruins, old, overgrown

houses, beautiful gardens, or an idyllic stretch of water. You can also, of course, walk through the Forêt de Blois.

Ménars. Eight kilometres upstream stands the Château de Ménars, one of the rare Baroque châteaux on the Loire. It was acquired in 1760 by the Marquise de Pompadour, mistress of Louis XV, and altered to the style of the period by the renowned architect Gabriel. The château is famous not only for its elegant interior but also for its terraced gardens which slope gently down to the Loire.

Vendôme and the valley of the Loir. It makes a pleasant change from the usual Loire route if you follow the course of the Loir, which is a northern tributary of the Loire and should not be confused with the Loiret near Orléans. You can reach the Loir by taking the D957 in Vendôme, 32 km from Blois.

The old town of Vendôme is dominated by the ruins of a 13th–15th c. fortress and is spread out over several islands formed by the arms of the river. The most significant building is the former *Abbey Church of the Holy Trinity* which has a magnificent Flamboyant façade. A walk through the *Quartier Ancien* should not be missed; it is as though time had stood still here.

If you follow the course of the Loir westward as it meanders through its wide river valley, you will pass through the following interesting places on the detour from the main region.

In *Lavardin* and *Montoire-sur-le-Loir* it is not so much the fortress ruins which will interest you as the astonishing Romanesque wall paintings in the village church and the *Chapel of St-Gilles* respectively. A large series of frescos from the period around 1200 may also be seen in the *Church of St-Jacques-des-Guérets* opposite Troo. But do not miss the sights along the river: old bridges and mills, weeping willows and wisteria, anglers, and washer-

women who still do their washing, as did their grandmothers before them, on a washboard in the river.

In *Poncé-sur-le-Loir* stands a small *Renaissance château* with a magnificent staircase. Not far away you will come to another château (which is not open to the public), the *Manoir de la Possonnière*, the birthplace of the poet Pierre de Ronsard. Again and again you see willows, alders, aspens, vines and reflections in the water — and also anglers. The Loir is considered one of the best-stocked rivers in France: perch, pike, trout, tench and eels are all caught here.

The river gradually begins to get wider and becomes less idyllic, but you can follow it as far as La Flèche. In order not to stray too far from the Loire, however, turn on to the N138 at Château-du-Loir and head for Tours (38 km).

Château de Ménars

From Blois to Tours

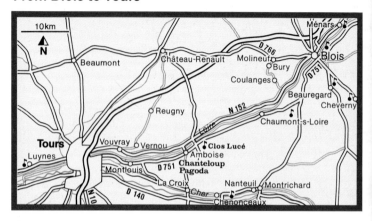

Much of what has made the Loire famous and interesting is concentrated between these two towns, on the southern side of the river and in the hinterland. Work out a route which will allow you to include the churches and châteaux, towns and scenery of your choice; this guide can only offer suggestions. Leaving Blois via the old bridge, turn right and after 21 km you will come to Chaumont-sur-Loire on the D751.

Chaumont-sur-Loire Alt. 65 m. Pop. 800
(Château de Chaumont: see page 71.)

 Hotel and restaurant: *Hostellerie Château.*

The road beyond Chaumont clings to the banks of the Loire and there is unspoiled river scenery to enjoy before you reach your next destination.

Amboise Alt. 57 m. Pop. 12,000
(Château d'Amboise: see page 74.)

Clos-Lucé, the manor house in the Rue Victor Hugo, has close connections with the château. Leonardo da Vinci spent the last three years of his life here as an honoured guest of François I; he died here in 1519. The country seat, with its beautiful garden, is lovingly maintained and tastefully furnished. You can see here models of machines constructed on the basis of da Vinci's original sketches. An unusual museum in the

Hôtel Joyeuse is the *Musée de la Poste* with its fascinating exhibits from the mail-coach era.

The Chanteloup Pagoda stands to the south of the town on the fringe of the Forêt d'Amboise. It is the only surviving part of a château built at the time of Louis XV and later demolished. The top of the 44-m-high pagoda can be reached by a flight of 149 steps. It was built in the Chinese style in 1775 in accordance with the tastes of that time. The panoramic view from the top of the pagoda is famous and well worth the long climb.

  Hotel and restaurant: *Château de Pray* on the road to Chaumont.

The D751 follows the banks of the Loire and continues to Tours via Montlouis, where a pleasant white wine is produced.

Between the Cher and the Indre

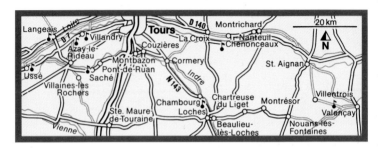

From Tours, take the D140 road and follow the Cher upstream. At La Croix the road from Amboise which traverses the Forêt d'Amboise comes in from the left. A little further on you pass through the village of Civray which has a rather plain Romanesque church. Even in the first half of the 19th c., at the time of Balzac, the Touraine countryside must have looked very much as it does today. It is 35 km from Tours to Chenonceaux (the name of the town is spelt with an x, but not the château).

Chenonceaux Alt. 62 m. Pop. 300
(Château de Chenonceau: see page 62.)

  Hotel and restaurant: *Bon Laboureur et Château.*

Before you reach the small town of Montrichard, 8 km from Chenonceaux, you come to the church of *Nanteuil* (12th–15th c.) which has long been a place of pilgrimage at Whitsuntide.

Montrichard Alt. 68 m. Pop. 4000
At the end of the 10th c. the powerful and warlike Foulques Nerra, Count of Anjou, had a castle built on this strategic site — the roads from Blois to Poitiers and from Tours to Bourges converge at this point — in order to bring the Cher valley under his control. The *donjon* which towers over the area was reinforced and its height increased at the beginning of the 12th c. in line with a similar example at Loches. You may climb the keep from where you will have a good view over the little town and the Cher valley. In the castle chapel at the foot of the hill the man who was later to become King Louis

XII married Jeanne de France in the year 1476. He then divorced her in order to marry Anne of Brittany, the widow of Charles VIII.

 Hotel: *Château la Menaudière.*

St-Aignan-sur-Cher Alt. 84 m. Pop. 3800
This town lies 17 km from Montrichard. At the end of the 9th c. monks from the Monastery of St-Martin in Tours built a chapel here which was much visited by pilgrims. It was rebuilt many times. The present *Church of St-Aignan* dedicated to Bishop Anianius of Orléans dates from between 1100 and about 1220; the porch tower and the crossing tower are particularly striking. The interior is acclaimed as one of the most impressive in any Romanesque ecclesiastical building in the Loire region. Some of the frescos in the crypt below the choir have been excellently preserved. The 'Christ in Majesty' in the apse chapel dates from the 12th c., and the scenes from the life of St Egidius are thought to be from the

beginning of the 13th c. Some old houses in the *Rue Constant-Ragot* and the view from the château terrace are also well worth seeing. The château itself, however, is not open to the public.

The road now takes us in a south-easterly direction away from the banks of the Cher. Quiet side-roads cross peaceful farming country, and a particularly fine stretch of woodland, beginning close to Villentrois, extends as far as Valençay.

The 'Christ in Majesty', St-Aignan-sur-Cher

Valençay Alt. 140 m. Pop. 3200
(Château de Valençay: see page 89.)

  Hotel and restaurant: *Espagne*, 8 rue Château.

Nouans-les-Fontaines. On the way to Loches you should have a look at the panel painting in the village church here. It dates from about 1470 and is the work of Jean Fouquet of Tours, the greatest portrait painter of his day in France. The picture, 'The Descent from the Cross', was clearly not originally intended for this modest little village church.

Montrésor. A *château* stands on the site of an earlier fortified castle built in the 11th c. by Foulques Nerra. The present building has been extended and modernised many times, and was finally restored in the 19th c. by a family of Polish aristocrats. Of more interest, perhaps, is the neighbouring *church* (1519–41), with its splendid doorway depicting gruesome decapitated figures, precise in every detail, from the time of the French Revolution, and also its tomb, to house which the church was originally built. This splendid Renaissance work, magnificently sculpted in white marble, was constructed by order of the Lord of Bastarnay for himself, his wife and his son.

Le Liget. The last place you come to on the way to Loches is Le Liget, a former Carthusian monastery and today an estate and private residence. The key to the *Chapel of St-Jean*, a Romanesque rotunda in the nearby wood, is kept here. Inside are frescos showing a Byzantine influence which were painted before 1200.

The Carthusian monastery was built by Henry Plantagenet to expiate the murder of Thomas à Becket in Canterbury Cathedral in 1170.

Beaulieu-lès-Loches. Continuing your journey you soon arrive at Beaulieu-lès-Loches where you can see the ruins of an *abbey church* founded in 1004 by Foulques Nerra. All that remains is an enormous Romanesque bell-tower.

Loches Alt. 72 m. Pop. 7000
(Château de Loches and Cité Médiévale: see page 76.)

Following a visit to the depressing castle dungeons in the keep, it is a good idea to have a stroll through the town, which has watch-towers, city gates, and handsome Renaissance buildings, such as the *Hôtel de Ville* and the *Maison de la*

Chancellerie. There is also a little park in which you can walk.

The Indre, which joins the Loire below Tours, is reached at Loches. From here you can drive back to Tours on a direct route (61 km), but the recommended round trip is extended in order to take in Azay-le-Rideau and Villandry.

The Indre valley, like the Loir valley (see page 33), is relatively secluded. There are, of course, a few tourists, but these are people who are not in a hurry to 'do' five famous châteaux each day, but who are content to discover something for themselves: a lovely half-timbered farmhouse, a gentle bend in the river which catches the light, a half-ruined mill with walls covered with wisteria, a meadow full of fruit trees, a shepherd surrounded by his flock, an angler sitting motionless in his boat. Every so often you will come across a Romanesque village church or the ruins of a medieval castle. Popular sights are few and far between, which makes this journey all the more relaxing.

Leave Loches on the N143 so that you can turn on to the quieter D17 at Chambourg and drive along the banks of the Indre.

Cormery. You have to get back on to the N143 in Cormery but can soon leave it again by making a left turn. There is an old *abbey* in the town dating from the 11th c. (the western end) to the 15th c.

Couzières. The D17 passes a château (not open to visitors) which stands in a large park. A little further on the road crosses the N10 at Montbazon and immediately afterwards passes under *L'Aquitaine,* the Tours–Poitiers motorway.

Montbazon is a pleasant little town and a popular holiday resort. Its landmark is the *keep,* the origins of which can be traced back to the great warrior and builder Foulques Nerra, Count of Anjou (about the year 1000). A path leads to the foot of the ruins. The route continues sometimes on the right and sometimes on the left of the Indre.

Pont-de-Ruan is a picturesque village which few can pass by without first having attempted to capture on film the idyllic atmosphere of river, bridge, country houses, mills and gardens. The journey from here to Azay-le-Rideau is equally charming on both sides of the river. Follow the southern route, however, so that you can visit the château which has connections with Balzac.

Château de Saché

The building dates from the 16th c. but is only noteworthy because the novelist Honoré de Balzac lived and worked here from time to time (and hid from his creditors here). Balzac, who was born in Tours, but was a Parisian by inclination, wrote 'Le Lys dans la Vallée' (The Lily in the Valley) here. It is set in the surrounding countryside.

Several rooms in the château have been devoted to Balzac and have furnishings from the period of his many stays here, as well as manuscripts, caricatures, original editions of his books and personal memorabilia. The literary associations and the 19th c. décor afford a welcome change after so many medieval fortresses and Renaissance châteaux.

It is a further 6.5 km to Azay-le-Rideau, but before you go there you should make a detour to Villaines-les-Rochers.

A special tip

Traditional basket-making is still carried on in the little village of *Villaines-les-Rochers*. You can watch craftsmen at work making baskets, chairs and other attractive goods, all of which are for sale.

Azay-le-Rideau Alt. 44 m. Pop. 2900
(Château d'Azay-le-Rideau: see page 80.)

After leaving the château you can see the *Church of St-Symphorien* on the left. It is an 11th c. building which was later extended.

From Azay-le-Rideau take the narrow D39 heading north towards the Loire.

Villandry Alt. 94 m. Pop. 700
(Château de Villandry: see page 78.)

  Hotel and restaurant: *Cheval Rouge.*

From Villandry you can either take the D7 back to Tours or follow a more pleasant route across the peninsula formed by the confluence of the Loire and the Cher. You can, of course, combine your visits to the châteaux of Azay-le-Rideau and Villandry with visits to Langeais, Ussé and possibly Chinon. A circular trip taking in all these châteaux can be made from Tours.

Azay-le-Rideau

Villandry from the château

The gardens at Villandry

Tours Alt. 48 m. Pop. 145,000
Tours is the most important and the largest town in the Loire Valley. The conurbation (pop. 250,000) extends considerably beyond the official limits of the town. Tours is the chief town of the Département Indre-et-Loire, the see of

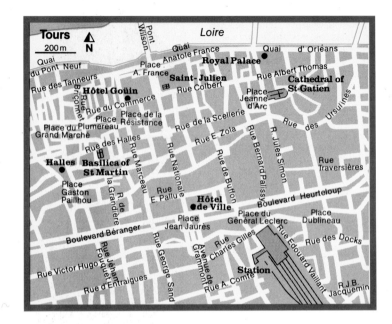

an archbishop, a university town, the
junction of several important routes, and
a tourist centre. It is the home of
important industries such as textiles,
electronics, chemicals and
pharmaceuticals, and many commercial firms are located here.
Consequently Tours has everything a
town in the French provinces could wish
for, with, moreover, an agreeable quality
of life. In France, Tours is regarded as
the town where the best French is
spoken.

There was originally a Gallic
settlement on the right bank of the
Loire. For reasons of security this was
transferred by the Romans to the narrow
tongue of land between the Loire and the
Cher, and called Urbs Turonum.
Christianity was brought to the region in
the 3rd c. by Bishop Gatien, to whom the
cathedral is dedicated, and was later
spread by St Martin. Following his death

in 397, St Martin of Tours, who as a
Roman soldier had shared his cape with
a beggar, soon became a legendary
figure. In the church which was built
around his tomb the Merovingian king
took a solemn vow, on St Martin's Day in
498, that he and his family would be
baptised. Thenceforth St Martin was the
patron saint of the Franks and their
kings.

Tours was a famous name in the
cultural and religious world of the early
Middle Ages. St Martin's tomb attracted
many pilgrims, and it was not long before
stories of miracle healing which had
taken place there became widespread,
and the number of pilgrims increased
still further.

A monastery founded in the 6th c.
close to the cathedral became highly
renowned when the famous Alcuin,
previously head of the palace school in
Charlemagne's court, was appointed
abbot in Tours. Here he established a

school of calligraphy which produced the most magnificent examples of medieval illuminated manuscripts.

For a time the Norse invasions brought this flourishing period to an end. The cathedral, the basilica and many other churches were set on fire and some were destroyed. Later followed the inevitable disputes among the feudal lords over this highly attractive property, until the town was finally taken over by the French Crown in 1242. King Louis XI, whose favourite residence was the Château de Plessis-lès-Tours (see page 43), introduced the manufacture of silk to the town, as a result of which the citizens achieved considerable prosperity. As elsewhere, the proud middle class in Tours had leanings towards Protestantism in the 16th c., and consequently suffered badly during the Religious Wars. A steady decline in the town's fortunes began after the expulsion of the Huguenots by Louis XIV, and this was halted only by industrialisation and the development of road systems throughout the country during the last century. The Old Town of Tours suffered heavy damage in 1940 and 1944 during the Second World War. Painstaking restoration work is still being carried out.

Stained-glass window from St-Gatien Cathedral, Tours

  Sights

The Old Town has two centres: the former Roman town around the St-Gatien Cathedral, and the so-called Châteauneuf around the Basilica of St-Martin.

In places the walls of the old *Roman town* are still identifiable, for example in the *Rue du Petit Cupidon* in the east and the *Rue du Général Meunier* in the south. Part of the western wall was used as the foundations of the cathedral towers. The dimensions of the Roman town seem surprisingly small by modern standards.

St-Gatien Cathedral. The building of the cathedral was begun in 1239 and construction work was completed in the 16th c. The top of the choir is early Gothic, the choir and the nave are predominantly high Gothic and the façade is late Gothic (Flamboyant). The cupolas on the towers are in the Renaissance style.

The *interior* has a powerful effect, with that clarity of line and proportion which belongs to the finest examples of the high Gothic style. The effect of height and space is enhanced by the glowing colours of the stained-glass windows in the choir and in the 13th–14th c. choir chapels. The rose windows in the north and south transepts likewise contribute to this effect. Also in the south transept is the touching marble tomb of the two children of Charles VIII and Anne of Brittany (about 1500).

Adjoining the cathedral to the north are the remains of the cloisters, known as *La Psalette* because, in addition to the library, the choir school (where psalms were sung) was housed here. The *Musée des Beaux-Arts* is in the former archbishop's palace which stands at the southern end of the cathedral. Paintings by Mantegna, Rembrandt, Rubens and Delacroix and furnishings from the period of Louis XV and XVI are on display.

Royal Palace. If you leave the cathedral and head straight for the Loire embankment you will come to the *Château Royal*. Practically all that remains standing is the 13th c. *Guise*

Vieux Tours restoration

Tower. The *Logis du Gouverneur* which adjoins it dates from the 15th and 16th c.; work is being carried out on its further restoration. A waxworks museum, the *Historial de Touraine*, is housed in the Guise Tower.

Returning a short distance and walking along the Rue Colbert you arrive at the *Place Foire-le-Roi* where some handsome 15th c. *gabled houses* and a 16th c. *Renaissance town house* can be seen.

The Church of St-Julien. Immediately before you reach the Rue Nationale you come to the Church of St-Julien. Although this former Benedictine abbey dates from the 13th c., it has modern stained glass windows, created in 1960 by Max Ingrand. The very interesting *Musée de Compagnonnage* (Museum of Journeymen) is adjacent to it. The Compagnons were medieval craftsmen who formed their own professional groups, which can be seen as the forerunners of the guilds. The museum, at 8 Rue Nationale, is devoted to the techniques and uses of medieval crafts which either have become extinct or are little practised today.

Vieux Tours. If you cross the Rue Nationale you come to the other quarter of the Old Town of Tours. It was once called Châteauneuf but is now known as *Vieux Tours*. The *Hôtel Goüin* in the Rue du Commerce is immediately noticeable. A town house in the Italian Renaissance style (1510) with a small garden at the front, it has been excellently rebuilt following its destruction during the Second World War. It houses the *Archaeological Museum* of Tours. Of greatest interest are the rooms in the basement which offer a detailed survey of the prehistoric, Gallic and Gallo-Roman periods. On the other floors are collections of items from the Middle Ages, the Renaissance and the period of French classicism.

Continuing along the Rue du Commerce you come to the *Place Plumereau*, a picturesque square surrounded partly by 15th c. half-timbered houses. This is the centre of Vieux Tours, restored following the havoc wrought by the last war. Notice the work, for example, in the Rue Briçonnet which leads from the square to the Loire. Perhaps not all the restoration has been a total success, but the general effect is in the main positive. Shops and inns, as well as market halls in the immediate vicinity, all ensure that the restoration forms part of a living environment.

Basilica of St-Martin. The Rue des Halles is reached via the Rue du Change. At this point you will be standing on the foundations of the old Basilica of St-Martin but there is almost nothing left of the building. The sole remains are the so-called *Charlemagne's Tower* (11th c.) in the Place de Châteauneuf and the *Clock Tower* (12th–13th c.), in the Rue des Halles, which has been masked by additions from later periods. The remains of the cloisters in the Rue Descartes date from the 16th c. The new Basilica of St-Martin was built in the Byzantine style between 1887 and 1924. The tomb of the saint may be seen in the crypt, and is still the destination for many pilgrims, especially on November 11th.

Place Jean Jaurès. This is the centre of the New Town where the *Hôtel de Ville* stands, a palatial building constructed in the ostentatious style of the later 19th c. The town's two large arterial roads cross each other at this square: from north to south the Rue Nationale and the Avenue de Grammont, and from west to east, laid out on the site of earlier defensive walls, the Boulevard Béranger and the Boulevard Heurteloup. Most of the hotels, restaurants, shops and specialist dealers are concentrated around this

square. In the *Maison de la Touraine* (4 Boulevard Heurteloup) local products from Touraine may be purchased: faience, silk goods, embroidery, books, pictures, wine, cheese, etc.

Château de Plessis-lès-Tours. This château stands to the west of the Old Town and is reached via the Quai du Pont Neuf and the Rue du Plessis. It was built in 1463 by Louis XI and became his favourite residence; he actually died here, in 1483. It is a plain brick building which contains furnishings and other items dating from the time of Louis XI.

St-Cosme Priory. The priory is quite close by. The choir and the ambulatory in the old church date from the 11th and 12th c. The refectory with its raftered ceiling is particularly fine; it is also worth having a look at the cloisters which have been transformed into a garden. There is a memorial to a former provost, the poet Pierre de Ronsard (1524–85), in the priory.

Hotels: *Bordeaux*, 3 Place M. Leclerc, near the station; *Akilène*, 22 rue du Grand Marché, Vieux Tours; *Château de Beaulieu*, on the road to Villandry.

Restaurants: *Barrier*, 101 Avenue Tranchée; *La Petite Marmite*, 103 Avenue Tranchée; *L'Antidote*, 39 rue du Grand Marché, Vieux Tours.

The Route to Vouvray

To reach the vine-growing region of Vouvray, where one of Touraine's best-known white wines is produced, leave Tours on the right bank of the Loire and continue a short distance upstream on the N152. There are several wine cellars in Vouvray where the wines may be sampled and bought. It is worth taking a trip from here on the D46 to Reugny, going via Vernou and passing through the valley of the Brenne.

From Tours to Angers

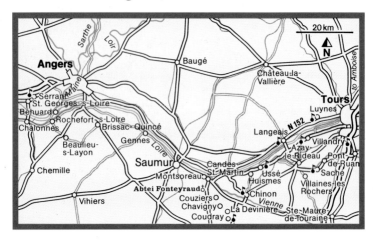

Leave Tours in a westerly direction on the N152. The road runs along the bank of the Loire. The opposite bank is a peninsula formed by the two rivers Loire and Cher which flow practically parallel to one another.

Luynes Pop. 4000

A defiant *fortress*, ancestral seat of one of the powerful medieval feudal lords in the Touraine region, overlooks this small town. The most impressive view of the castle, which is not open to the public, can be obtained if you go into the town and climb the opposite slope up to the cemetery. The two outer round towers on the west side may well date from the 13th c. and the two central ones from the early 15th c.

It is quite likely that there was an encampment on this strategic hill as long ago as the Gallo-Roman period. Indicative of this are the preserved arches of an aqueduct 1.5 km to the north of Luynes.

Langeais Alt. 53 m. Pop. 4100
(Château de Langeais: see page 82.)

This little town lies in the once fiercely disputed border regions of the counts of

Luynes

Angers and Tours, which is why one of the oldest of the medieval fortresses on the Loire was located here.

The route now follows the southern side of the Loire. If you turn left you come to Villandry (see page 78) and back again to Tours. If you keep straight on you will come to Azay-le-Rideau (see page 80). Immediately beyond the bridge bear right, however, and drive along a pleasant stretch of road following the Loire, on an embankment which protects the neighbouring farmland against flooding. There are attractive views on both sides of the road. At this point the Indre flows for some distance alongside the Loire before the two rivers unite.

A road sign points the way 'inland' to Ussé. The best view over the whole château complex is from the bridge which crosses the Indre.

Ussé
(Château d'Ussé: see page 90.)

Continue via Huismes and along the fringe of the Forêt de Chinon to Chinon. This town may also be reached direct from Tours via Azay-le-Rideau (48 km).

Chinon Alt. 37 m. Pop. 9000
(Château de Chinon: see page 65.)

From the château hill a footpath leads steeply down into the town of Chinon, which extends in a long narrow strip between the foot of the hill and the Vienne. The path will take you to the *Grand Carroi* which is both the market place and the lively centre of town. Houses dating from the early Middle Ages (some even from the 11th c.) still stand here, as do many from the 15th–17th c. They are very decorative and make a picturesque scene. The pedestrianised area formed by the Rue Haute St-Maurice and the Rue Voltaire will fascinate all who stroll through it. There are half-timbered buildings, oriel windows, and overhanging upper storeys.

Chinon

A plaque on the house at 44 Rue Voltaire, in the Place St-Maurice, refers to important historical events which did indeed take place on this site but not in this actual building. In 1199 Richard the Lionheart is supposed to have died here in a tower room having been badly wounded at the siege of Châlus, and in 1428 the site was the meeting-place for the States General summoned by Charles VII. For that reason this house is known as the *Maison des Etats Généraux* and has been equipped as a museum which contains, among other items of interest, relics of the stake at which Joan of Arc was burned.

The town's network of underground caves and passages is not open to visitors. The existence of these caves has been associated with numerous legends and anecdotes, but in reality at least they have proved effective as places of refuge, air-raid shelters and wine cellars.

You can get a splendid view of the town and the château from the Quai Danton on the other side of the Indre, after crossing the bridge, some of whose piers date from the 12th c.

🛏 🍴 Hotel and restaurant: *Château de Marcay*, 7 km to the south of Chinon on the D116.

La Devinière. Keep to the south of the Vienne and follow the signs to La Devinière (taking the D749, 751, 759 and 117). There is a house here in which the satirist François Rabelais (1494–1553) spent his childhood. It is a plain mansion, modest in size, with a worn outside staircase and a pretty orchard bordering on fields and meadows, probably just as it did in Rabelais' time. It has been converted into a museum which contains many exhibits relating to Rabelais and his times, and in particular to Gargantua, the hero of his vast work.

The tales which Rabelais related of Gargantua, Pantagruel and his other heroes play an exceptional role in French literature. They form a Celtic-Gallic counterbalance, as it were, in a literature which had otherwise been dominated by classicism. Since the scene for Gargantua's adventures is set on the Loire, there can be no pleasanter quest for the admirer of Rabelais than to seek out those locations where the action takes place.

Fontevrault Abbey

Continue to drive through the pleasant countryside of rolling hills — on the left is the Château de Coudray on a hillside — and through the sleepy villages of Chavigny and Couziers to Fontevrault Abbey.

At the end of the 11th c. an abbey was founded here which soon became so popular that it was extended into five separate complexes: a monastery, a convent, a leper colony, an infirmary and a home for fallen women. An abbess was appointed to take overall charge. The counts of Anjou generously supported the abbey with large donations, and when they later became the Plantagenet kings of England chose it as their burial place, thus honouring it as the principal abbey in the whole of their sovereign territory. The abbesses were invariably of noble birth and many were princesses. Fontevrault therefore became not only one of the largest abbeys in France, but also one of the richest, which was not always good for its reputation. From time to time Christian morals in the abbey did decline. Further difficulties, and much suffering, were experienced during the Revolution. The buildings were plundered and some parts were burned to the ground; the occupants were driven out and murdered or guillotined. Napoleon downgraded the abbey, making it a prison, which it remained until 1963, since when extensive restoration work has been in progress.

📷 You enter the abbey through a porch. On the left is the stable block, which the last abbess built at great expense before the Revolution. The other buildings around the stable-yard date from the 18th and 19th c.

The *abbey church*, one of the most impressive Romanesque churches in Anjou, was consecrated by Pope Calixtus II in 1119. The emptiness of the interior creates an extraordinarily severe effect. The domed ceilings, which are most striking, are more typical of south-western France (Périgueux). On the side walls of the nave you can still see the places where mezzanines were installed during the last century for the accommodation of prisoners. In the south transept there are four tombs with recumbent painted effigies (restored) dating from the 12th and 13th c: Henry Plantagenet, Count of Anjou and King Henry II of England; Eleanor of Aquitaine, his second wife; Richard the Lionheart, their son; and the fourth figure is thought to be that of Isabelle of Angoulême, Queen of England, who died a nun in Fontevrault in the year 1246.

Chinon

Saumur

The two cloisters, *Cloître Ste-Marie* (16th c.) and *Cloître St-Benoît* (17th c.), and the huge Gothic refectory with its rib vaulting can also be seen, together with the adjoining Romanesque abbey kitchen. This 27-m-high octagonal construction was separated from the other buildings so that no inconvenience was caused by the odour of cooking coming from it. The kitchen has not been restored to exactly the original design, but it is still possible to appreciate the skill with which the builders designed the fireplaces, flues and air vents.

Candes-St-Martin Alt. 37 m. Pop. 270

From Fontevrault you can drive on a narrow back-road to Candes-St-Martin where the Vienne flows into the Loire. St Martin died in this town in the year 397, and in 470 the first church was dedicated to him here, although his mortal remains had been buried in Tours. The church which now stands on this site dates from the 12th and 13th c. The doorway is lavishly decorated with figures, and the so-called Angevin vaulting inside is worth seeing.

The calcareous rocks which appear on the south bank of the Loire between Montsoreau, beyond Saumur, and the region of Gennes were quarried for the traditional building materials for churches and châteaux. Numerous fossils estimated to be 80–100 million years old have been found here. The caves which have been carved out of the rock are also used as wine cellars for the Saumur wines which benefit from the constant temperature and humidity.

Recently the caves have been used for the cultivation of mushrooms, which has developed quite favourably here. Seventy per cent of the French mushroom harvest is produced in the Saumur region; up to 300 tons are picked daily from the underground passages which cover approximately 800 km.

Saumur

A special tip

On the left bank of the Loire below Saumur (D751) you can visit the *Louis Bouchard Mushroom Museum* housed in a rock cellar. Here you can learn everything there is to know about the cultivation of mushrooms.

Saumur Alt. 30 m. Pop. 34,000
(Château de Saumur: see page 84.)

During the early Middle Ages the town was fiercely contested by the counts of Anjou and Blois, a situation which lasted until Saumur was brought under royal ownership by Philippe Auguste. Following the Reformation, and particularly during the reign of Henri IV, Saumur became a recognised Protestant stronghold. Trade and commerce flourished and a Protestant university was founded here. When the Edict of Nantes was revoked in 1685 by Louis XIV two-thirds of the population left the town. Many of them settled in Brandenburg, Prussia.

Saumur sank into provincial decline until the foundation of the Cavalry School in 1767 assisted its recovery. In 1972 the National Equestrian School, which trains civilian riding instructors, was transferred to Saumur. Large and prestigious riding displays and parades attract many enthusiasts throughout the year.

In addition to the *Museum of the Horse* in the château, there is a *Cavalry Museum* in the Avenue Foch which contains some impressive exhibits. Cavalry troopers were renowned for being first-class soldiers and great importance was attached to their being smartly uniformed.

Of the churches in the town *Notre-Dame-de-Nantilly* is the finest and most worth visiting; it is a single-naved Romanesque building with barrel vaulting, and was extended and modified in late Gothic Flamboyant style during the 15th c. Louis XI's *oratory* is today used as a baptismal chapel. The church contains a fine collection of tapestries from the 15th–16th c.; eight of them, depicting scenes from the life of Christ, are from Aubusson (17th c.).

  Hotel and restaurant: *Le Prieuré*, in Chênehutte-les-Tuffaux, 8 km downstream.

End of July: displays by the *Cadre Noir* (an elite French cavalry unit) from the cavalry school, which is steeped in tradition.

Continue to Angers either on the D952 (45 km) or on the D751.

Angers Alt. 47 m. Pop. 143,000
(Château d'Angers: see page 86.)

Angers, the former capital city of Anjou, lies on the Maine, a short yet important river, which is formed by the confluence of the Sarthe and the Mayenne and which flows into the Loire 10 km further south. It is a lively town with a southern air about it. A certain cosmopolitanism which can be detected among its inhabitants might be explained by the town's historical past. The House of Anjou, a significant power in France as long ago as the 10th c., had dynastic ties with southern Italy and England during the Middle Ages.

The duchy of Anjou, fiercely fought over for centuries by France and England, was finally united with the French Crown by Louis XI in 1481. Unlike Tours or Saumur, Angers was scarcely affected by the Reformation, and was therefore able to develop comparatively undisturbed. Today wine production and the wine trade, textiles and the electronics industry are the important economic factors in the town and its suburbs. The extraction of slate, the manufacture of liqueurs and the cultivation of vegetables also play a significant role. The Anjou Festival, held during June and July, with numerous performances of theatre, music and dance, as well as art exhibitions and poetry readings, is considered the most important cultural event, after the Avignon Festival, in provincial France.

Sights
The heart of the city is bordered by wide boulevards which form a rectangle adjacent to the Maine. Rising in the south-western corner of this rectangle is an enormous fortified castle with seventeen towers.

To reach the town centre from this fortress, go down the Rue Toussaint. A little road on the right leads to the *Logis*

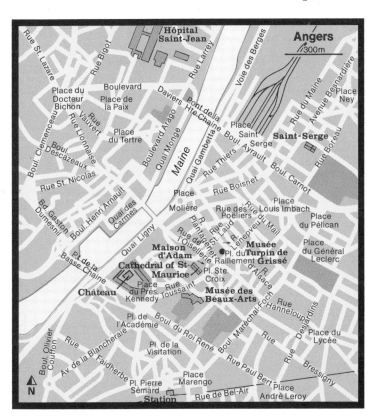

Barrault, a 15th c. mansion which now houses the *Musée des Beaux-Arts*. French 18th c. painters including Watteau, Boucher and Fragonard are well represented here. Return to the Rue Toussaint and proceed to the *Place Sainte-Croix* where there is a building which must surely . be the most photographed in the town. The *Maison d'Adam*, built about 1500, is an exquisite half-timbered house richly decorated with wood carvings.

The Cathedral of St-Maurice. Towering above the square is the cathedral, a building constructed mainly during the 12th–13th c. A central tower, crowned by a cupola, was added to the twin-towered façade in 1535. The sides of the doorway are richly and interestingly decorated with Romanesque biblical statues. In the tympanum there is a figure of Christ in Majesty, with the symbols of the four evangelists. Statues of St Maurice and his militant followers stand in recesses above the central window.   Unfortunately,   these sculptures have been badly mutilated.

The nave of the cathedral is unusually wide — 16 m instead of the more usual 9–12 m. One of the earliest examples of Gothic Angevin vaulting (about mid-

St-Maurice Cathedral, Angers

Maison d'Adam, Angers

12th c.), which is of great architectural interest, can be seen here. The keystones of the pointed arches are some 3 m above the level of the transverse arches and are a typical feature of this kind of vaulting. The stained-glass windows in the choir and the transept, with their warm red and mystical blue tones, are extremely fine. Scenes from the lives of St Peter, St Eloi (patron saint of smiths) and other saints are represented. The rose windows in the transept depict 'Christ in Majesty' and 'Christ the Man of Sorrows'. (Explanatory notes about the various motifs can be found in the choir.)

Place du Ralliement. This square is the hub of the town. Another stately mansion, the *Hôtel de Pincé* (1525–35), stands at the point where the Rue Lenepveu branches off from the square. The *Musée Turpin de Crissé* is located in this house, and collections of Greek and Etruscan vessels, as well as art from East Asia, are on display. More fine houses from the 15th and 16th c. may be seen in other streets of the Old Town such as the Rue de l'Oisellerie, the Rue des Poëliers, and the Rue Saint-Laud, which also has some most attractive shops. The two buildings described below, which are outside the Old Town, are also worth viewing.

The Church of St-Serge. This church, which does not look very impressive from the outside, is well worth visiting if you are interested in architecture. The choir is representative of the Angevin style of around the year 1200, that is, in its most beautiful and developed form. The keystones and corbels, over 100 in number, illustrate the theme of the Last Judgement and are quite outstanding.

Hôpital St-Jean. One of the oldest infirmaries still preserved was established on the other side of the Maine during the 12th c. The hospital ward, 60 m long and 22 m wide with three aisles, is vaulted by a ceiling in the Angevin style and is very impressive. This, together with the altar in the main aisle, is symbolic of the fact that in the Middle Ages the sick were tended more from a spiritual than a medical standpoint. The ten modern tapestries (1957–66), known as *Chant du Monde*, by Jean Lurçat, are an attempt at creating a modern version of the Apocalypse theme, inspired by the Apocalypse tapestries in the Château d'Angers.

 Hotels: *Anjou*, 1 Bd. Maréchal-Foch; *France*, 8 Place de la Gare.

Restaurants: *Le Quéré*, 9 Place du Ralliement; *Le Toussaint*, 7 rue Toussaint; *Brasserie du Grand Cercle*, 18 Bd. Maréchal-Foch.

Mid-June to mid-July: *Anjou Festival* with performances of theatre, music and dance, art exhibitions and poetry readings.

 South of Angers

Leave the town in a southerly direction and take the D748 to *Brissac-Quincé* (18 km). Two round towers are all that remain of a 15th c. fortress on the site of which the *Château de Brissac* was constructed at the beginning of the 17th c. The well tended grounds and luxuriously furnished interior are well worth a visit.

Narrow roads take you through vineyards and meadowland to the picturesque wine-producing town of *Beaulieu-sur-Layon*, where the elegant *Hôtel Desmazières* comes into view. Via Rochefort-sur-Loire you can get to the island of *Béhuard*, on which there is a church, in the middle of the old village, which was endowed in the 15th c. by Louis XI. The interior is well worth seeing.

Return towards Rochefort and take the narrow *Corniche Angevine*, a road which twists and turns with marvellous views until it reaches *Chalonnes*. Those with an interest in geology will notice that the Loire and its branches cross the divide here between the soft calcareous rock which has been in evidence until now and the hard rocks which from now on flank the river on its way to the sea. Vineyards, fields of tobacco plants, and sheep pastures dotted with broom bushes line the route. The Loire flows on, wide and majestic, forming islands here and there which have been inhabited for centuries by farmers and fisherfolk. Occasionally you will see windmills, some of them restored and others practically in ruins.

From Chalonnes, cross the Loire on the D961 back to the north bank. The *Château de Serrant*, surrounded by a wide moat, stands close to the road leading out of *St-Georges-sur-Loire*. Although the construction of the château spanned the three centuries from the 16th to the 18th, the style is harmonious. The rooms are beautifully furnished and contain examples of everything which in its day was expensive and of good quality (Flemish tapestries, Venetian mirrors, rare books, etc.).

Drive back to Angers on the N23 (18 km).

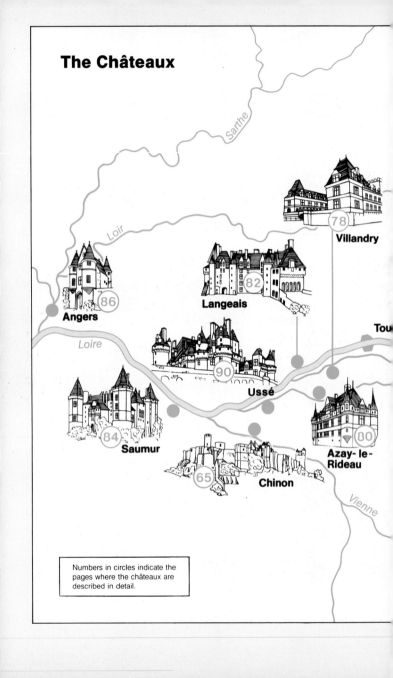

The Châteaux

Sarthe

Loir

78
Villandry

86
Angers

Loire

82
Langeais

Tou

90
Ussé

84
Saumur

65
Chinon

80
Azay-le-Rideau

Vienne

Numbers in circles indicate the pages where the châteaux are described in detail.

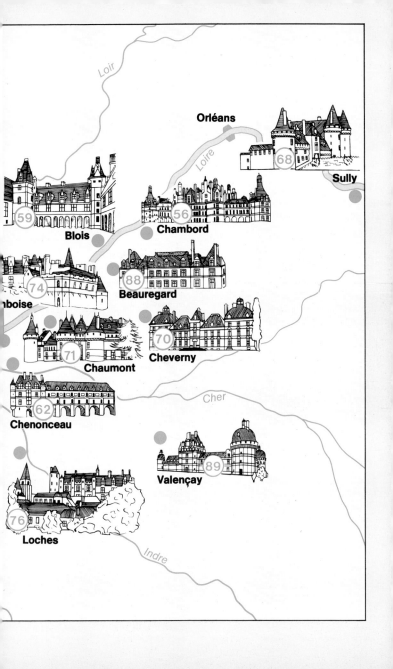

Orléans

68

Sully

59

Blois

56

Chambord

74

88

Beauregard

Amboise

71

Chaumont

70

Cheverny

62

Chenonceau

Cher

89

Valençay

76

Loches

Indre

Loir

Loire

Chambord

Chambord is the largest, most extravagant and most famous of all the Loire châteaux, but opinions vary widely about whether it can be regarded as the finest in France. The château arouses surprise and wonder in its visitors. One of the first, the Emperor Charles V, is supposed to have called it 'the epitome of human achievement in art'. However, unlike Chenonceau and Azay-le-Rideau, Chambord does not arouse a feeling of affection.

Commissioned by François I, the construction of the château began in 1519. At that time the king already had his residences in Blois and Amboise, but now wished — as a true Renaissance prince — to have a château which would specifically represent him, his power, his rank and his fame.

For that purpose only the best and most expensive was good enough. Money was no object. He set about achieving his aim in a devious way: debts were not paid, church treasuries were plundered, vassals were blackmailed and heavy taxes were imposed on townsmen and farmers alike. The king did not care – the main thing was that building should continue.

Following his defeat at the Battle of Pavia in 1525, François was taken prisoner and held captive by the Emperor Charles V in Madrid for a year. On his return to France one of his first official acts was to speed up the work on the château. When he died in 1547 it had still not been completed. Building was continued under the direction of his son and heir, Henri II, but after a time, when it was still not finished, work stopped. It was not until Louis XIV came to the throne that the terraces and chapel tower, at least, were completed. Chambord was planned on too large a scale ever to be finished.

It is said that François only spent a total of forty days at Chambord, but his dream had become a reality and his posthumous fame was ensured. In 1577 the Venetian ambassador declared, 'I have seen many splendid examples of architecture in my lifetime, but never a more magnificent or more opulent creation. The park in which the château stands is filled with woods, lakes, streams, meadows and hunting grounds. And towering up in the centre of all this is a beautiful building with gilded pinnacles, lead-roofed wings, pavilions, terraces and galleries....We are leaving the place full of wonder, amazement, even dismay.'

But how does one use such an enormous building which has been left unfinished? It was originally intended to be a hunting lodge in the Forest of Boulogne which is rich in game, and stag hunting and falconry were organised from time to time. But civil war and the Huguenot Wars in the second half of the 16th c. meant that kings had little time for diversions of this kind. From the reign of Henri IV the Court resided in Paris, and the rooms of the château were only rarely filled with hunting parties after that. Louis XIV and the whole royal household visited Chambord on several occasions, and Molière was allowed to perform two of his comedies there. Finally, in the 18th c. Louis XV placed the Chambord estates at the disposal of the Marshal of Saxony, for services rendered on the field of battle. The marshal was a stickler for discipline. He brought with him two cavalry regiments and kept them occupied with army exercises. Anyone who failed to conform to the strict régime was immediately put to death on the gallows. The fact that the marshal occasionally had a play performed in the château did not make him any more popular.

Château de Chambord

Five avenues lead through the *Forest of Boulogne* to Chambord. From whichever direction you arrive you see the château rising up out of the woodland at the end of the avenue, an impressive first sight. The forest is vast but does not give the impression of being overwhelmingly large. The largest part (5500 ha.) belongs to the Park of Chambord and is a state reserve for hunting deer and wild boar. It is surrounded by a 32-km-long wall which could well be the longest one in France.

The château stands, surrounded by parkland and meadows, on the re-routed course of the Cosson. François I even conceived the idea of having the Loire diverted to flow past Chambord, but fortunately his technical advisers were able to dissuade him. The building has a rectangular ground-plan and is 156 m long and 117 m wide, with 440 rooms, making it the largest château on the Loire. Its north-west façade on the Cosson is the most attractive, but entry to the château is through the *Porte Royale* in the south-east, which looks more like the rear entrance, as it is here that the building remains in its most unfinished state.

When you enter the *Court of Honour* you get a general view of the castle

The staircase

floor the stairs open out on to four large rooms, which are disposed in the form of a cross around the staircase. It is quite likely that Leonardo da Vinci, who was at the court of François I in Amboise at the time the château was being planned, provided the technical solutions to some of the constructional problems. The guides accompanying the tour describe in detail the furnishings and fittings in the rooms on the various storeys. But one should not forget, in admiring the details, to appreciate the harmony of the whole.

The same applies to the roof terrace to which the staircase leads. A miniature fairytale town has been built on it which has fascinated visitors for centuries.

'We move around among rectangular and cylindrical buildings of all sizes, carved from stone and richly decorated with diamond shapes, triangles, circles and semicircles which in reality represent towers, turrets, side turrets, chimneys, dormers and niches. The whole is adorned with shells of all kinds, flowers, nymphs, fauns, sphinxes, handsome monsters and a joyful band of winged cupids. The royal emblems appear everywhere: lilies mainly, singly or in groups, and the letter 'F' in all sizes. There are royal crowns and salamanders breathing fire....' (Champigneulle.)

This fairytale town on the roof of the donjon, with an almost oriental appearance, was not merely created to satisfy an idle delight in displays of splendour. It is clear that the king wished to offer something to a household forced to follow him into the solitude of the hunting grounds on the edge of the Sologne: change, amusement, and an opportunity for relaxation with games of hide-and-seek, to help cavaliers and coquettes while away the boredom!

layout: a huge rectangle with four corner towers surrounding a square building (also with four corner towers), one side of which forms part of the façade — a typical ground plan of a medieval fortress. But in the case of Chambord even at an early stage it was realised that such a format was no longer relevant. Certain forms, however, outlive the purposes for which they were designed, and so do certain names; the square tower, for instance, is still known as the *donjon* (keep).

The donjon is the core of the château and a highlight of French Renaissance architecture. The staircase, which is of Italian design, is really two spiral staircases in one, and is so constructed that people going up can see those going down, but are not able to meet. On each

Blois

Blois is a name associated with the murder of the Duke of Guise. However, the graphic descriptions given by the château guides do not accord too closely with historical fact. But if you are interested in the development of architectural styles on the Loire between the Middle Ages and the period of classicism, they are nowhere better displayed than here.

The sizeable estate of the counts of Blois was acquired in 1391 by Louis, Duke of Orléans, brother of Charles VI. His son, Charles d'Orléans, was taken prisoner by the English at the Battle of Agincourt in 1415. He was a poet, and it is said that only poetry gave him the strength to endure his twenty-five years of imprisonment. When he was finally allowed to return to his beloved Blois, he had part of the medieval fortress demolished and replaced by a building which was more comfortable to live in. He held court here and entertained his literary contemporaries, among them François Villon. When he was seventy years old he fathered a son who later became King Louis XII.

Louis XII made Blois his royal residence and he and his wife, Anne of Brittany, furnished it according to their taste. The reign of Louis XII was a comparatively good period in the history of France. More famous, however, is his successor, François I, who was brilliant, adventurous, untrustworthy, ambitious and a lady-killer, and made heavy demands on the French, in both blood and money. History is not always a fair judge! François I was constantly on the move with his enormous royal household between Blois, Amboise and Chambord — when he was not engaged in war in Italy, or held prisoner by Emperor Charles V in Madrid.

The kings who succeeded him also often changed their residences, but to the extent that one can speak of a capital of France in the 16th c., this was undoubtedly Blois. The States General gathered here in 1576 and 1588 in order to lodge complaints or to express wishes to the king. The Duke of Guise, who was the most powerful and popular man in the realm at this time, brought pressure to bear on the king to hold the second meeting, his purpose being to depose the weak Henri III and to have himself proclaimed king. The vast majority of the members of the States General supported him, but the king was aware of the plot and — with the approval of his mother, Catherine de Médicis — twenty noblemen armed with swords and daggers, who still placed their hopes in the king, murdered the duke during the meeting of the council. However, the king had a clear conscience. He wrote to the French Ambassador at the Holy See, 'I am convinced that he [the Pope] will praise my action, as it is not only permitted but also right to secure the peace of all men through the death of a single person.' Following the subsequent murder of the duke's brother, the Cardinal of Lorraine, those who had formed a strong opposition to the king were executed, and the king was able to set about making arrangements with the legitimate successor to the throne, Henri de Navarre. When the king himself was murdered a year later — an act of revenge by a Guise supporter — Henri de Navarre was able to ascend the throne almost unchallenged. As Henri IV he became a great figure in French history. With him began France's most splendid era, the 'Great Century', in Paris. The Loire had played out its historical role.

Like Henri IV, whom he succeeded, Louis XIII had no affection for the Loire châteaux, and he exiled his brother,

Château de Blois, Louis XII Gate

Gaston, a constant troublemaker and conspirator, to Blois. In order to steer him away from his intrigues he provided him with the means for reconstructing the entire château. Later, when Gaston was no longer a danger, funds were withheld and the reconstruction remained unfinished. Gaston, made wiser by age and exile, devoted his time to the natural sciences, collected rare plants and laid out a huge garden in the grounds of the château.

📷 It is not necessary to join an official guided tour of Blois. Armed with one of the leaflets provided, you should be able to look around the château on your own. Viewed from the Place du Château, the *façade* is divided into two parts. On the right is the *Salle des Etats Généraux* (13th c.), the only remaining relic of the medieval fortress, and adjoining it is the *Louis XII Wing* (around 1500), built of ashlar and brick and with asymmetrically placed windows. Above the late Gothic main entrance is an *equestrian statue of Louis XII*, together with his heraldic device, the porcupine.

If you look back towards the entrance when you enter the *inner courtyard* of the château, you will see the Salle des Etats Généraux to the left and the Louis XII wing in the centre. The courtyard appears to be an irregularly shaped rectangle and is open only on the west. In much of what you can see here you will sense a relaxed Italian ambience; the many-shaped arabesques in the arcades have without doubt been imported from across the Alps. Museums are housed in the wing today – a *Religious Art Museum* and a *Fine Art Museum* containing mainly paintings. The *Chapel of St-Calais* which adjoins it was consecrated in 1508. This consists only of the choir from a larger church which was torn down during the construction of the Gaston d'Orléans Wing. It has recently been restored having been badly damaged by bombing during the Second World War. The modern stained-glass windows are the work of Max Ingrand who also created those in the chapel of Amboise (see page 74).

The most startling architectural feature of the château viewed from the inner courtyard is the *François I Wing* situated between the Salle des Etats Généraux and the Gaston d'Orléans Wing. The newly crowned king began the conversion of the wing in 1515, although the core dates from an earlier period. The loggias on the town side and the façade overlooking the courtyard, with the famous staircase tower, were generally regarded as a triumph for the new style of architecture. Much was left incomplete, and symmetry could not always be observed; some detail has been more freely worked than the strict Renaissance style permits, but it is all the more invigorating. The *staircase tower*, with its elegant form and extravagant décor, is a really fine work — a masterpiece of the 16th century. It has lost something of its effect, however, as it is no longer in the centre of the façade because of the building of the classical wing.

The *Gaston d'Orléans Wing* was designed in 1635 by Mansart, the most famous architect of his day (and creator of the mansard roof), but the classical style of the 17th c. has the effect of being dull and almost boring in comparison with the lively, inspired forms of the early Renaissance. Gaston d'Orléans had originally intended to demolish the old château completely; fortunately lack of money prevented him from doing so.

In the François I Wing the staircase (the guard of honour was positioned on the tiny balconies) leads up to the first floor where you can see several grand fireplaces and also the royal couple's heraldic devices which occur again and again — the salamander of François I, and the swan of his wife, Claude.

The porcupine — heraldic device of Louis XII

Although he did not hold her in particularly high esteem, she nevertheless bore him seven children in eight years. She died at the age of twenty-four. In the room known as the *Cabinet of Catherine de Médicis,* which is panelled throughout, you can see cupboards with secret compartments which can be opened only by means of a pedal in the skirting board. It is often said, although not proven, that the Queen Mother kept here the poisons which were intended for those in disfavour. The bedroom in which Catherine died, next to her private chapel, may also be seen.

On the second floor are the three rooms where the murder of the Duke of Guise is supposed to have taken place. The guides point out exactly where Henri III was sitting, where the murderers waited for the duke, and which route he tried to take to get away. The pictures on the wall portray the sequence of events through the eyes of 19th c. artists.

Before leaving the château you will pass through the Salle des Etats Généraux, the oldest part of the complex, where the States General assembled in 1576 and 1588.

Chenonceau

Chenonceau is neither the largest nor the most historically significant of the Loire châteaux but it is probably the best loved. Resplendently cheerful, it rises up from its watery surroundings at the end of an avenue of plane trees. There has been no bloodshed here; royal celebrations have been held, and doubtless plots hatched, but the sad events which have inevitably occurred here only form a dark backcloth against which the Renaissance shines forth all the more brilliantly.

At the beginning of the 16th c. Chenonceau was sold by an aristocratic family in need of money to Thomas Bohier who as treasurer to the French kings had come into a fortune. The old castle was pulled down and a château in the modern Italian Renaissance style was built in its place. Only the keep remained standing. As Bohier had no choice but to accompany the sovereign on his Italian campaigns, the direction of the building project lay primarily in the hands of his wife, Catherine Briçonnet. A woman's influence is perhaps evident in the practical way in which the living rooms are arranged around a common vestibule, and in the kitchens and other domestic rooms in the basement (1513–21).

The Bohiers, however, were not able to enjoy their splendid château for long, and after they died it was taken over in 1526 by King François I who thus felt compensated for the fact that his minister had been vigorously helping himself to funds from the public exchequer. In 1547, Henri II on his accession to the throne presented the château to his mistress, Diane de Poitiers.

Diane must have been an extraordinary woman; the painting in the Louvre which depicts her as the goddess of hunting walking naked through the woods (Fontainebleau School) reveals something of her mystery. She was almost twenty years older than the king but nevertheless continued to enthral him to the end of his days. Contemporaries praised her smooth white skin and delicate complexion. One of them even went as far as to say that at seventy she could have been taken for a thirty-year-old — and that was without make-up! That was a slight exaggeration, however, as she died when she was sixty-seven.

Diane was not only devoted to her royal master but also to the Château de Chenonceau. She commissioned the building of the five-arched bridge gallery over the Cher and had the large rectangular garden in front of the château laid out. This was originally an ornamental garden together with an orchard and kitchen garden. Neither the Archbishop of Tours nor any other ambitious gentleman could refuse when Diane requested gifts of precious plants.

It goes without saying that the king did not fail to give his support, and it is said that he introduced the bell tax to please her; twenty *livres* per bell were payable annually, most of which was passed on to her, giving rise to the sarcastic comment by the writer Rabelais, 'The king has hung all the bells in his realm around the neck of his mare!'

For twelve years Diane was able to enjoy the favour of the king and the beauty of her château. Most of all — so it was whispered among her contemporaries — she loved to plunge naked at sunrise into the Cher, and then climb onto the back of a waiting white stallion and ride off like the wind into the distance. When the king was killed in 1559 at a tournament, the mourning widow, Catherine de Médicis, who had on several occasions been humiliated because of Diane, found time the

Château de Chenonceau

following day to relieve the now defenceless favourite of all her jewels. Immediately afterwards she was banished from the Louvre and she was later forced to give up her beloved Chenonceau in exchange for Chaumont (see page 71).

In triumph Catherine, the king's widow and the mother of three future kings (François II, Charles IX and Henri III), made her appearance at Chenonceau. It was said at the time that her rival's possession of the château had hurt her almost as much as her possession of the king's heart. Chenonceau now became the scene of noisy gatherings at which not only did the pompous self indulgence of the courtly company play a role, but so did their pleasure in making veiled remarks of a rather risqué nature. The re-enactment of naval battles, firework displays, lavish classical stage performances with nymphs and satyrs, tournaments, jousting competitions,

battues, balls, concerts and banquets all took place here.

Catherine had a two-storeyed gallery built over the bridge wing, as well as various domestic buildings, and had her own private park laid out to the south-west of the château. Further plans for extension which would have made Chenonceau the largest of all the Loire châteaux never materialised. After Catherine's death, her daughter-in-law, Louise of Lorraine, widow of the murdered King Henri III, inherited the château and spent the rest of her life there in deep mourning. She came to be known as 'the inconsolable'. The château is now privately owned.

📷 Chenonceau is one of the few châteaux on the Loire which may be viewed without a guide. Just by looking out of the windows you can appreciate the enchanting interplay of architecture, parkland, water and riverbank. First of all you come to the terrace surrounded by a moat, with the old *residential tower*, and then by crossing over a further bridge you arrive at the main building. The *vestibule* has late Gothic rib vaulting but elsewhere in this wing, which was commissioned by Catherine Bohier, the Italian Renaissance style is dominant. To the left is the former *guardroom*, from where the chapel and a small terrace which overlooks the Cher may be reached. Adjoining it is *Diane's Room*, which has a very fine fireplace by Jean Goujon. Although the Flemish tapestries here and in the guardroom date from the 16th c., they do not form part of the original furnishings. Adjoining this room are the *Green Cabinet* and the little *library*, both with their original ceilings (wooden-beamed and coffered respectively) dating from the time of Catherine de Médicis. The two rooms to the right of the anteroom are named after François I and Louis XIV. Have a look at the two large fireplaces as well as the paintings: 'Diane de Poitiers as the Goddess of Hunting' (Primaticcio?), 'The Infant Jesus with St John' (Rubens?), 'Portrait of Madame Dupin' (Nattier) and a magnificently framed portrait of Louis XIV by Rigaud.

Leading to the upper storey is one of the first straight 'Italian' staircases in France. This type took over from the spiral staircase which had been customary up to that time. The four rooms in the upper storey were decorated and furnished later in the style of the 16th c. Be sure not to miss the kitchens and other domestic rooms in the basement. The waters of the Cher rush by quite close to the small rooms at the side, reminding you that the first building on this site was a water mill.

Viewed from the outside, the adjoining two-storeyed gallery of Catherine de Médicis built over Diane de Poitiers' bridge appears to be out of proportion, yet the room which you enter creates a splendidly cheerful impression, mainly due to the light which streams in on both sides. A commemorative plaque records that the gallery was used as a military hospital during the First World War. In the Second World War it served as part of an escape route used by members of the French Resistance trying to reach the unoccupied part of the country which began on the south side of the Cher.

If you take a walk through the park you can enjoy the beautifully laid out grounds and appreciate from every perspective the unparalleled situation of the château. In one of the domestic buildings is the *Musée de Cires* (wax museum) where fifteen scenes from the history of Chenonceau are depicted.

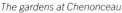

The gardens at Chenonceau

Chinon

Although Chinon is included among the Loire châteaux, it might be better described as a fortress. The building was not intended to be stately. It has always been first and foremost a fortress, from where the ruler could force his will upon the province and to where he could withdraw when he needed to defend himself.

The long, rocky spur above the Vienne offered the best natural prerequisite for a fortified castle. A *castrum* stood upon the site as long ago as the Gallo-Roman period. The castle, built in the 10th c. by the counts of Blois, fell into the hands of the counts of Anjou in 1044. Their successors in the House of Plantagenet — the English kings Henry II and Richard the Lionheart — extended and further fortified the building in the 12th c. In August 1205, after a siege lasting eight months, the French king Philippe II succeeded in capturing the castle from the English. It continued to be a residence of the kings of France up to the end of the reign of Charles VII.

Chinon's moment of glory came in the spring of 1429. It was here that Joan of Arc met the weak Charles VII, then known as the Dauphin (successor to the throne) because he had not yet been crowned in Rheims. Joan's request that Charles should set about reconquering the regions occupied by the English was the beginning of a memorable chapter in French history, which marked a decisive turn in the Hundred Years War (see page 12) and gave the French a sense of patriotism.

Differing accounts of the meeting on February 25th 1429 have been recorded — depending on whether Joan, in the opinion of the chronicler, was a charlatan, even a witch, or a messenger sent by God. The eighteen-year-old country girl from Lorraine was presented to the king — who had long delayed receiving her — in a hall where 300 inquisitive, sceptical and mocking dignitaries had gathered. In order to test the girl, the king hid himself among his courtiers; it is said that he even exchanged clothes with one of them in order to mislead her. But Joan, as modest as she was self-assured, recognised her king, genuflected before him and said, 'My Lord Dauphin, I have been sent by God to assist you and the kingdom of France.' In another version, when asked by the king who she was, she is supposed to have replied, 'My name is Joan the Maid, and the King of Heaven sends you word through me that you will be anointed and crowned in Rheims and the King of France will become the servant of the King of Heaven.' This scene and all the historical events which are supposed to have taken place as a result have been interpreted in various ways. It is only possible to relate the straightforward facts here. The king was inclined to place his trust in Joan but first she was brought before a kind of court of inquisition in Poitiers, in order to dispel any doubts that she might be a tool of the devil. Her reactions left the most malicious of her adversaries dumbfounded. She returned to Chinon and was provided with a small army. On April 20th she set off to defeat the English and to liberate Orléans (see page 14).

Under Charles VII's successors, Chinon came into the limelight only briefly, on one occasion. In 1498 the papal legate Cesare Borgia brought permission from the Pope enabling King Louis XII to divorce his wife, Jeanne, so that he could marry Anne of Brittany. She was the widow of his predecessor, Charles VIII, who had bequeathed her to him in his will. Louis was fonder of her than he was of his wife, who was

The château, overlooking the town

deformed and whom he had been compelled to marry at the age of fourteen.

After that the château fell into decay. In 1633 it came into the possession of Cardinal Richelieu whose family also allowed it to fall into disrepair. It was only in the 19th c. that the château came to be regarded as a historic monument, worthy of preservation.

📷 Situated on a rocky spur, the fortress is 400 m long and about 70 m wide. It is divided into three parts which are separated by moats and connected to each other by bridges: the *Château du Milieu*, with the royal apartments; adjoining it to the west the *Château du Coudray*; and to the east the *Fort St-Georges*.

Entry to the Château du Milieu is through the gate in the *Tour d'Horloge* (clock tower). The narrow, rectangular-shaped 14th c. tower, where on the roof platform the *Marie Javelle bell* still strikes the hours, is quite remarkable. In the north-east corner of the château is a round tower in which there is a small and somewhat uninspiring *Joan of Arc Museum,* spread over three storeys.

On the way to the *Grand Throne Room* you will get a wonderful view over the town of Chinon and the Vienne valley to the south. You will have to imagine, however, what the throne room would have looked like when Charles VII received Joan of Arc. The west gable wall with its huge chimney piece on the first floor and some exterior walls are all that remain.

Adjoining this are the fairly recently reconstructed *Logis du Roi* (royal apartments). In one of the rooms there is a picture of Agnès Sorel who was the mistress of Charles VII, and indeed the first official mistress of a French king. Agnès, the 'Dame de Beauté', lived in a small mansion at the foot of the castle hill which was connected by an underground passage to the royal apartments.

Below the royal apartments were the armoury, kitchen, wine cellars and staff quarters. All that is left of the rest of the Château du Milieu is parts of the walls and ruined towers; yet the château stimulates the imagination and the visitor can easily picture the magnificent setting filled with knights and their ladies.

Crossing a bridge, you come to the Château du Coudray with its three prominent towers: the 12th c. *Mill Tower* on the exposed south-western corner; the *Tower of Boissy* which dates from the 13th c. and from whose platform there is a panoramic view; and the keep, the *Donjon du Coudray,* also dating from the 13th c., with walls over 3 m thick in the lower part. At the beginning of the 14th c. members of the Order of the Knights Templar were incarcerated here on the orders of the king before being brought to trial in Paris, where the majority of them were burned at the stake. The inscriptions on the walls in the middle storey of the tower are said to be by the knights.

Before leaving the château, have a quick look into the *Fort St-Georges*. It was constructed in the 12th c. in order to protect the actual castle at the point where it was most easily accessible. Apart from some modest remains of the exterior walls, only the *crypt* of a Romanesque chapel has survived.

Right: Tour d'Horloge

Sully

Sully is the first of the 'classic' Loire châteaux and to some extent an introduction to the many which follow — both downstream and along the tributaries. As most visitors begin their Loire trip in Orléans this château has fewer visitors than it deserves.

Sully is a moated château, surrounded on all sides by arms of the Sange, a little tributary of the Loire. A fortress which controlled one of the most important of the Loire crossings stood here in the 9th c., if not earlier. In its present form the château dates mainly from two different periods. The medieval castle was built in the 14th and 15th c. (there is a carpenter's bill dated 1363 to prove it). The enormous keep, flanked by four corner towers, forms the centre of the château and gives it its unmistakable military character.

The Renaissance addition dates from the beginning of the 17th c. The building was commissioned by Maximilien de Béthune, who bought the château from the de la Trémoille family and who is known in French history by the name of Sully. A minister under Henri IV, Sully was not only a loyal servant of the king but also a statesman of outstanding quality. In recognition of his many services the king honoured Sully with a dukedom.

Sully, who at the age of twelve had entered the service of Henri de Navarre (who had not yet become king of France), held many offices: chamberlain, privy councillor, inspector of fortifications, grand-master of the artillery (he was considered the best authority on artillery of his time, and established France's leading position in this field), and minister of finance, agriculture and industry. 'He combined within himself the soul of a farmer with that of a lawyer and created what till then had been lacking not only on the banks of the Loire but throughout the whole of France: a system through which the royal will was executed by lawful means.' (Champigneulle.)

In 1610 Henri IV was assassinated by the fanatic Ravillac, and Sully was forced to retire to his home on the Loire as a political pensioner. He renovated and extended the château, had an embankment built to protect the property from flooding and enlarged the park. Yet these activities did not keep him fully occupied. By all accounts his capacity for work was phenomenal. He rose at daybreak and kept four secretaries busy recording his memoirs. Since they were written in the elaborate Baroque style of the time, however, they are almost illegible today. Also contained in them — as a kind of political testimony to his king — was the wholly modern concept of a united Europe which would live in eternal peace, where conflicts would all be settled and customs barriers raised. He was just a few centuries ahead of his time with this idea.

Sully, however, had his faults. He had a passion for money. And even on his estate he liked to maintain a kind of personal 'royal household' and was insistent that strict court etiquette should be observed. He thus retained a number of loyal minor noblemen and a lifeguard one hundred strong. His pedantry, however, bordered on the bizarre. It has been recorded that he insisted on drawing up legal contracts for even the most banal of everyday arrangements — probably because he was so cantankerous and enjoyed subjecting his peers to legal actions which sometimes lasted for years!

The *keep* towers over the inner courtyard and is reached via the outer courtyard and the bridge (formerly

Château de Sully

a drawbridge). Work started on the donjon about 1360. The guardroom, kitchen and chapel are on the ground floor. The *hall* on the first floor is occasionally used for concerts, but in the 18th c. the young Voltaire, banished from Paris, performed plays here which he had written in the park — a thank-you to his host, who had offered him a comfortable and convenient place of refuge in Sully. Next to the hall there is a small *chapel* which contains a copy of the double tomb of the Duke of Sully and his wife.

On the second floor is the *Great Hall* with its magnificent open roof timbers which are considered one of the finest examples of medieval carpentry in existence. The construction in chestnut-wood is in the form of an upturned boat. The excellent state in which the timbers have been preserved is a result of the extraordinarily careful preparation of the material. Only tree-trunks fifty to one hundred years old were used. They had previously been stripped of their bark right down to the heartwood before being felled in the winter. The finished beams were then laid in water for months until all the sap had been drawn out, and they were then air-dried. Finally the timbers were so arranged that air was able to reach them from all sides. The result is that the roof timbers show no sign of age and no damage by woodworm, and as there is no dry rot to attract flies there are not even any cobwebs.

The *Renaissance wing* of the château has the Duke of Sully's study on the ground floor and his bedroom in the upper storey. The restoration of the wooden ceilings and the tapestries has not been particularly successful.

Cheverny

This late-comer among the châteaux on the Loire was not subject to the various influences of the Renaissance period. As a result the ground-plan of the château is symmetrical and the exterior somewhat cold-looking. It is only the different types of roof above the individual sections of the building which break up the severity of the classical style. In comparison with Chenonceau or even Blois the stylistic unity of the building is very striking. Its construction took only a few years, and hardly anything has been altered since its completion in 1634. After changing hands several times the property and its large park have come into the possession of an indirect descendant of the builder, Count Henri Hurault.

The dominant style here is that of the Louis XIII period and one gets an excellent impression of the lifestyle of the aristocracy of that time. It is quite apparent that the lady of the house furnished her rooms tastefully and that wealth and taste went hand in hand. There is some beautiful furniture in the rooms on the ground floor and in the gallery: the chairs are upholstered with Aubusson tapestry work, and on the walls are Flemish tapestries designed by David Teniers, as well as panelling depicting love scenes, in grisaille painting. You can also see family portraits — the finest, which hangs above the fireplace in the Grand Salon, is by Mignard — and paintings from the workshops of Titian and Raphael.

A splendid carved *staircase*, richly decorated, ascends to the upper storey, where you can see the *guard room* with its magnificent fireplace and an interesting panel depicting flowers against a landscape background in green grisaille. Adjoining this room is the *King's Bedroom*. Here you are almost overwhelmed by the profusion of different colours and forms: beneath a coffered ceiling, with illustrations from the story of Perseus and Andromeda, there is a state bed, and sumptuous wall tapestries with scenes from the 'Odyssey'.

The present occupant of the château also owns a large hunting ground and his deer hunts, which take place in the autumn, have become important social occasions. You can see the pack of eighty hounds which are used in the hunt, and there is also a *Hunting Museum* with huge numbers of antlers.

Château de Cheverny

Chaumont

Château de Chaumont (MOB-CRTL)

The name Chaumont is popularly said to derive from *chaud mont* (hot hill); the derivation from *calvus mons* (bald mountain) would also be apt. The fine park with its enormous old cedars, rising above the bank of the Loire, was not laid out until the 19th c. Nevertheless it has effectively disguised the once bare hills, and such hills now exist only in the surrounding countryside.

Two fortresses have stood upon the cliff above the Loire, one dating from the 10th c., the other from the 12th. Both were reduced to their foundations. The family which had the third building, the present château, constructed can be considered as representative of the non-royal aristocrats among the château-builders of the Loire. In the 15th c. Pierre d'Amboise, together with other feudal lords, rose up against the young King Louis XI, who as punishment for their unruliness had the medieval fortress razed to the ground. Shortly afterwards, however, Pierre d'Amboise was pardoned and was at once able to start building a new château (1465). His son, Charles d'Amboise, Marshal of France, admiral, and Lord Chamberlain to Louis XII, inherited the building, and construction was completed in 1511, the year of his death. Because of his duties for the king, he was forced to spend long periods away from the château and so he was assisted by his uncle, Georges d'Amboise, who was both a cardinal and, in effect, Prime Minister of France.

In 1560 Henri II's widow, Catherine de Médicis, acquired the château and forced her rival, Diane de Poitiers, to exchange her beloved Château de Chenonceau (see page 62) for Chaumont. Diane, however, refused to live here and moved back to her other château, Anet. During the following centuries the château changed hands several times. In the 18th c. the north range of the enclosed four-wing building was pulled down so that the owner at that time could enjoy from the courtyard the fine view of the distant Loire landscape. Soon afterwards the building came into the possession of a certain Le Ray from Paris who established a manufacturing workshop here. This proved most successful, especially as he engaged an Italian designer, G.B. Nini, who, working in a converted dovecot, produced ceramic medallions

with portraits of leading figures on them. It was thanks to this workshop that the château survived the French Revolution unscathed.

The Château de Chaumont experienced a 'romantic interlude' in 1810; it was made over to Madame de Staël as her place of residence when she had been forbidden by Napoleon to live within forty miles of Paris. She gathered a circle of literary figures and *beaux esprits* around her, including Benjamin Constant, August Wilhelm Schlegel, Adalbert de Chamisso and Madame Recamier, famous for her beauty and wit.

 Strolling under the overhanging cedars, you approach the château along a pretty little path through the park. At first sight it looks like an impregnable fortress, especially about the drawbridge, behind which there are two massive towers bearing the coat-of-arms of the d'Amboise family on their walls. In fact these towers are not really defensive structures at all. The frieze which decorates the lower part of the towers consists of two intertwined initials, both C (Charles de Chaumont), alternating with blazing hills (*chaud*

The drawbridge, Chaumont

The stables and pottery kiln, Chaumont

mont). On the frieze below the battlements are Diane de Poitiers' initials and emblems — hunting horn, bow and quiver. Above the gateway are the initials of Louis XII and Anne of Brittany on a background of lilies and ermine.

Of the other two towers, the west one (on the left), the *Tour d'Amboise*, is still a genuine fortified tower. It dates from 1465 when the new building was started and must have been intended as the last refuge in the event of a siege. On the other hand a magical aura surrounds the east tower (on the right), the *Tour St-Nicolas*. Catherine de Médicis is supposed to have withdrawn here with her astrologer, Ruggieri, in order to consult the stars about the personal and political fate of herself and her three sons.

Visitors who enter the *inner courtyard* are immediately drawn to the slope from where there is a commanding view of the Loire valley. Parts of the château's inner façades have been restored over the centuries, not to their advantage. The interior decoration has also been altered by its many owners, with the obvious intention of making the château more comfortable. The wall hangings and furniture date mainly from the 16th–18th c. The most splendid item of all is the Italian floor in the *Salle du Conseil*, made of faience tiles.

Next you see the luxurious *stables* which the Prince de Broglie built for his beloved horses 100 years ago on the site of Nini's workshop. The former dovecot in which the medallions were fired still stands as part of this complex.

Amboise

Of all the Loire châteaux, Amboise is perhaps the most difficult to reach, and owing to the ravages of time and man's destructiveness only fragments and reconstructions can be seen today. However, the splendid view over the river valley — as far as the steeples in Tours — and the château's history more than compensate for this.

Loire bridges and the fortresses which protect them are complementary, and in Amboise this link can be traced back to the Gallo-Roman period. Around the middle of the 15th c. the medieval castle belonging to the counts of Amboise was confiscated by Charles VII for the French Crown. Louis XI, who preferred the more unpretentious château of Plessis-lès-Tours, designated Amboise as the residence of his wife, Charlotte of Savoy. Here she gave birth to the Dauphin who in 1483 at the age of only thirteen ascended the throne as Charles VIII after the death of his father.

It was he who began the series of French campaigns in Italy in order to pursue his rather doubtful claims to the Crown of Naples. This 'Italian obsession' lasted for only a few decades and ended in total failure during the reign of François I. Culturally, however, France benefited greatly from its confrontation with Italy, and it was Charles VIII who brought with him to the Loire the first 'immigrant workers' from the south — architects, landscape gardeners, artists, decorators, etc. It was he who brought the Italian Renaissance to France and by so doing shaped the cultural development of the country during the following century.

In 1492 Charles VIII began work on his Château d'Amboise, forging ahead with great impatience. In 1498, however, the king died following an accident: he cracked his head on a lintel and passed away a few hours later on a sack of straw.

Soon afterwards the six-year-old François d'Angoulême came to the château with his family, and spent the rest of his childhood here. He was crowned king in 1515 and made Amboise the stage for a succession of feasts, balls and jousts. When building work on the château was complete, he invited Leonardo da Vinci to the Loire (see page 34). However, the surroundings laid out by his predecessors no longer satisfied François I who wanted his own château, one which would overshadow anything in existence at that time, and this was to be Chambord (see page 56).

A gruesome, bloody event occurred in 1560 which caused Amboise to figure once again in French history. Huguenots formed a conspiracy to withdraw the young François II from the influence of the Catholic Guise family, in Blois. They were betrayed and the king fled to Amboise, where the conspirators themselves were imprisoned. A massacre followed during which the Huguenots were beheaded, hanged or drowned — a spectacle which the king, his wife Mary Stuart, and the Queen Mother, Catherine de Médicis, could not miss!

First you come to the terrace which in the 16th c. was completely surrounded by buildings. Then you enter the inner courtyard which was the scene of brilliant open-air entertainments. The *Chapel of St-Hubert* now stands isolated on the ramparts, but it used to be a private chapel in the queen's section of the château. It was originally built in the late Gothic Flamboyant style but parts of the chapel were restored during the 19th c. Above the doorway there is a particularly fine rectangular relief depicting St Christopher and St Hubert. The figures

Château d'Amboise

in the reconstructed tympanum show Charles VIII and Anne of Brittany praying to the Virgin Mary. The windows in the chapel are modern and represent scenes from the life of St Louis. The remains of Leonardo da Vinci are supposed to be buried in the north transept.

Of the original trapezium-shaped complex all that now remains standing is the *Logis du Roi* on the Loire side of the château. This was built in the reign of Charles VIII but has undergone reconstruction. The wing which adjoins it at right angles and looks down over the terrace was built during the reign of François I. The rooms in this section are now furnished in a variety of styles, with some very handsome pieces dating from the 15th and 16th c. The most imposing room in the château is the rib-vaulted *Great Hall*, where the king received his guests whilst he was in residence in Amboise. It was here too that the Huguenot conspirators were imprisoned in 1560 before being executed on the balcony. Adjoining the Logis du Roi is the *Tour des Minimes* which also served as an entrance to the château from the Loire embankment. It has a spiral ramp which could be negotiated by horses and carriages. The tower is 21 m in diameter; from its upper platform there is a fine view of the surrounding area, as well as of the adjoining buildings.

Loches

Loches, a massive fortress in the upper part of the little town of the same name, rises from a rocky plateau commanding the Indre valley. Its early history is very similar to that of Chinon (see page 65): the castle of the counts of Anjou was fiercely fought over by the Plantagenet kings of England and the Valois kings of France. Richard the Lionheart captured it in a surprise attack in 1195, and in 1205 Philippe II (known as Philippe Auguste) reconquered the fortress for France following a lengthy siege.

Joan of Arc and Agnès Sorel, the two women most associated with Charles VII's reign, have both left their mark on Loches. After Joan of Arc and her small army had liberated Orléans from the English, she met the king in Loches and he was grateful to her and satisfied with her achievements. But Joan knew that her mission was not yet complete. *'Fille Dé, va, va, je serray à ton ayde, va!'* ('Child of God, go, I shall help you, go!') the heavenly voice had said to her, and she knew that meant that she must conduct the king to Rheims so that he could be anointed and crowned there, for only then would he truly be king. In Loches, she pressurised Charles, the weak procrastinator, and his ever doubting, mistrusting advisers, to risk the march to Rheims, and she succeeded. On July 1st 1429, seven weeks after the siege of Orléans, the coronation of King Charles VII took place in Rheims.

Years later Agnès Sorel arrived at the royal court in Chinon (see page 65). Her beauty and wit so captivated Charles VII, who had not himself been particularly well endowed by nature, that he took her as his mistress *en titre* (the first official favourite of the French court), and she bore him four children. However, the Dauphin, who later became Louis XI, hated and despised her, and as a result she moved back to Loches and lavishly endowed the clergy with gifts so that she could be buried in the collegiate church. She died in 1450. The clerics then suddenly had misgivings about allowing the 'sinner' to be buried in consecrated ground, but the king said that in that case they could return all her gifts. Agnès Sorel was buried in the church!

During the following centuries, the fortress had a less glorious existence as a state prison, a dungeon and a torture chamber.

The walls of the fortress form an irregular oval about 460 m long and 130–220 m wide. They also enclose the *Cité Médiévale* and the former collegiate church. It is worthwhile taking a walk around the entire complex either before or after viewing the château. By doing this you will get a vivid impression of the immense importance of fortresses such as Loches during the period when the feudal lords were constantly warring with each other.

Entry to the fortress is through the *Porte Royale*, a 13th c. building set between two round towers which date from the 15th c. On the way to the Logis du Roi you will see on your left the *Musée Lansyer* where there is a collection of landscape paintings by this 19th c. artist.

The *Logis du Roi* consists of several buildings. The older wing with its stout towers and connecting fortified wall-passages still reflects the fact that its sole purpose was a defensive one. In the wing which was added in about 1500 it is clear that Renaissance characteristics were beginning to intrude into Gothic structures. The adjoining tower is named after the beautiful Agnès Sorel.

It was in the *Great Hall*, according to tradition, that Joan of Arc managed to persuade the hesitant Charles to go to

Château de Loches

Rheims. The effigy of the recumbent Agnès Sorel is now preserved in the *Charles VIII Room*. Her body lay in the collegiate church before the French Revolution, but the church was badly damaged at that time. After two restorations there is probably very little of the original tomb left. The most notable room is the *Prayer Chapel of Anne of Brittany*, the walls of which are decorated with ermine tails — the heraldic device of Brittany — and with Franciscan knotted cords.

The *Church of St-Ours,* with its four pointed towers, has a somewhat unusual appearance. The two middle towers are hollow eight-sided pyramids with which the nave was vaulted over in the 12th c. The church was built between the 11th and 15th c. It has some magnificent early Romanesque sculptured decoration, especially on the capitals and the doorway in the porch

where there are scenes depicting the Adoration of the Magi. The fresco in the 11th c. crypt shows St Brictius, who succeeded St Martin as Bishop of Tours.

The *Donjon*, the fortified building at the southern end of the Cité Médiévale, protected the castle at its most vulnerable point. The donjon, 37 m high on a rectangular ground-plan, dates from the end of the 11th c. and is still recognisably of Norman origin. Fireplaces and window openings in the walls mark the three storeys of the tower, which once also served as a refuge.

The two other towers — *Tour Ronde* and *Martelet* — were used mainly as torture chambers and prisons. The most famous prisoner was Lodovico il Moro, Duke of Milan, who died on the day of his release. You will probably be glad to escape from the oppressive atmosphere of the Martelet's lower floors and to return into the daylight.

Villandry

The medieval fortress was purchased in 1532 by Jean le Breton, a Cabinet Secretary to François I. Everything except the massive keep was pulled down and rebuilt as a Renaissance château. Three wings arranged at right angles around an inner courtyard open out on the north to the Cher and the Loire. The old keep forms part of the complex, and the medieval moats have also been preserved. Several living-rooms, a dining-hall with Baroque panelling, and the great staircase are on show to the public.

🄯 Villandry is visited mainly for its unique *gardens*, which have a history of their own. The Italian pleasure garden was introduced into France at the same time as the Renaissance style of architecture. Contemporary engravings by Jacques Androuet du Cerceau, the royal landscape gardener to François I, give some idea of this type of garden. Following changing fashions most of these gardens were converted into English gardens over the centuries, with 'naturally formed' large stretches of meadowland and groups of trees. This is what happened at Villandry. In 1906, however, the château was acquired by Dr Carvallo, a Spanish physician, and it is thanks to him that an authentically styled, if not original, Renaissance garden exists here once more.

Dr Carvallo studied the old engravings by Androuet du Cerceau, called to mind the Moorish horticulture he had seen in Andalusia and had the English gardens ploughed up. Many old trees had to be felled and this caused an outcry, but his plans for the reclaimed area were put into effect.

He created three levels using the natural fall of the land. On the lower level he laid out a vegetable garden, on the central level an ornamental garden and on the upper level a water garden. A reservoir of 7000 square metres feeds the garden and the moats from here. The three levels are connected to each other by ramps and steps. The entire area is best viewed from the terrace on the east side.

You can stroll through these gardens, admire the curious yew trees which have been trimmed into various shapes, and enjoy the scent of the flowers and the view of the village of Villandry with its simple Romanesque church. But this would not do justice to the ornamental garden, in particular, which has a sort of programme. The geometric and symbolic shapes of the box hedges, which are exactly and carefully positioned on the gravel, represent different kinds of love. Pink roses framed by heart shapes signify tender love; hedges trimmed in the shape of swords and filled with red flowers signify tragic love; love run wild is represented by misshapen hearts and mixed colours; and fleeting love is demonstrated in the form of butterflies' wings and fans, and predominantly yellow flowers. These love symbols were current in the Renaissance period, but they have their origins in the medieval tradition of courtly love.

It is perhaps easy to understand flowers being used as symbols of love, but it seems strange for ordinary crops such as lettuces or cabbages to be used to create patterns. In fact it follows the tradition of vegetable gardens in medieval castles: apart from their usefulness they also had to be pleasing to the eye and impart a sense of confidence and courage in the event of a siege.

The vegetable garden of Villandry is a huge rectangle divided into nine plots intersected by paths. Each of the plots has a different pattern and much thought went into the selection of the plants to provide contrasting colours,

ranging from various shades of green to reds and violets. The vegetables are surrounded by flowers and at each corner there is a rose arbour. The author René Benjamin reported how Dr Carvallo explained his vegetable garden to him. 'I saw only flower beds. "That is because", said the doctor, "the vegetables look good between the flowers and the fruit, as they would on the table of a Frenchman with good taste. The squares consist of vegetables, but the flowers around them create their own effect; in addition, fruit trees grow in the corners of each square. Everything has been arranged in a strict geometrical pattern, expressing pure intelligence. Everything has its place and the whole is surrounded by an attractive little hedge."'

Top: Château de Villandry
Above and right: The gardens at
Villandry

Azay-le-Rideau

Together with Chenonceau, Azay-le-Rideau is one of the most charming and most visited of the Loire châteaux. Neither is a fortified castle with forbidding walls, but a country house where it was possible to live a normal life. They are not too large, but conceived on a human scale; and they are built on (and in) the river, so that the architecture which is very light in character is reflected in the idyllically peaceful water. Another possible reason why Chenonceau and Azay-le-Rideau are particularly charming is that although both were financed by rich men they were planned and furnished largely by their wives.

Azay-le-Rideau

The early history of Azay-le-Rideau was anything but peaceful. A fortress did, in fact, stand here in the Middle Ages and in 1418, when France was going through a difficult period during the Hundred Years War, it was occupied by a garrison of Burgundian soldiers, at a time when Burgundy was in alliance with England. When the Dauphin, who later became King Charles VII, wished to quarter his men here during a march from Chinon to Tours, the Burgundians jeered at him. The offended prince took cruel revenge: he stormed the fortress, burning it to the ground and massacring the entire garrison of 350 men. For a long time afterwards the place was known as Azay-le-Brûlé (the burnt Azay).

At the beginning of the 16th c. the property passed to a typical representative of the French *nouveaux riches*. Gilles Berthelot was one of the many public servants whose sole task was to supply the extravagant King François I with the funds he needed. The means by which this was achieved was of no interest whatsoever to the monarch, provided the money kept flowing in and appearances were more or less kept up. From time to time, however, these senior administrative officers and treasurers were called to account — as was Berthelot. With his cousin Semblançay, who was employed in the same capacity, he became involved in the embezzlement of public money, and this was discovered by the court auditor. When Semblançay was hanged Berthelot decided to flee, and the château, still not completed, was seized by François I and passed on to a loyal follower. (Balzac, who came from Touraine and lived from time to time at the Château de Saché close by, gives a humorous account of this event in his 'Contes drolatiques'.)

Azay-le-Rideau

The château was built between 1518 and 1529. Berthelot, who was fully occupied by his financial duties, left the planning and supervision of the building operations to his wife, Philippe, née Lesbahy, who decided to build the château on oak piles in the river-bed of the Indre. Four wings with an inner courtyard were originally planned, but it remained an L-shaped, two-winged building. In walking around the outside of the château the visitor will find that the final result proved more successful than the original plan as the perspectives are more varied and interesting.

The transitional nature of the architecture is clearly recognisable on the outside. Many elements are still essentially Gothic, with apparently defensive features such as towers, battlement walk and arrow slits, yet the building as a whole has an entirely Renaissance air about it.

This applies even more to the inside. The *staircase* with its double windows immediately attracts attention. It was one of the first of its kind in the country, the old spiral staircase having been replaced by straight flights, and shows the beginning of a development during which the stairway was to become an imposing central feature. The staircase at Azay has a fine coffered ceiling, with medallions showing the profiles of the kings and queens of France from Louis XI to Henri IV.

Even the *kitchen* has kept its original appearance, apart from the floor, which was raised at one time as the cooks complained that they needed boats to work from because of the frequent flooding. The kitchen has a rib-vaulted ceiling, parts of which have been decorated with humorous little scenes of life below stairs. The original fireplace is of interest, as is the draw-well which is fed directly from the Indre.

The remaining rooms in the château form a kind of museum of 16th and 17th c. interior decoration. On show are choice tapestries and carpets, furniture and paintings, and a number of restored fireplaces.

The Château d'Azay-le-Rideau is best viewed from the park. Its magic unfolds as you look at it from a distance through groups of trees and across the surface of the water. It is easy today to share the feelings Balzac experienced some 150 years ago: 'I first admired the Château d'Azay from a hill. Built on piles which were hidden by flowers, it was like a polished diamond framed by the Indre.'

Langeais

Château de Langeais

Langeais stands on the site of a Gallo-Roman fortified settlement which even in those days held a position of military importance. The next fortress was built at the end of the 10th c. Foulques Nerra, Count of Anjou, an extremely belligerent feudal lord, made it into a strategic base from where he could extend his power over Tours and Blois. All that remains of this building is part of the rectangular *donjon*, in the park above the castle. It is the oldest still to be seen in France and one of the first post-Roman stone constructions in the country. Defensive towers had previously been built of wood. During the following centuries possession of the fortress was constantly disputed between the counts of Anjou and Tours, and on occasions between England and France. The counts of Anjou were of course the Plantagenet kings of England, while Touraine was regarded as the heartland of the kings of France. At the beginning of the 15th c. the English handed the fortress over to the French against payment of a ransom, on the condition that it should be razed to the ground.

In 1465 Louis XI instructed his treasurer and Cabinet adviser, Jean Bourré, to build a new fortress, again for strategic purposes. The king thought

that Langeais would serve as an excellent barrier against the rebellious dukes of Brittany who, it was feared, might try to advance their frontiers further eastwards via Nantes and Angers.

Bourré carried out the building work within a few years, hence its unity of style. At the same time, it is the typical product of a transitional period: it is a fortified castle with high walls, battlement walks, defensive ditches and a forbidding approach over a drawbridge, and yet it has the potential for a comfortable Renaissance château lifestyle. The compromise in favour of more home comforts was to prove justified. Louis XI, who was just as disagreeable as he was clever and tenacious, finally succeeded through a marriage contract in uniting France and Brittany, which was a major accomplishment. For Anne of Brittany, who was at the centre of it all, was already engaged to the 'last knight', Maximilian of Austria, who later became Emperor, and it was clear that the marriage would unite the duchy of Brittany with the House of Habsburg, which would have been a disaster for France. The marriage contract was dissolved, however, and Anne was able

One of many historic attractions in the château

to marry Charles VIII, son and heir to Louis XI. To ensure a lasting bond between the two powers it was written into the contract that Anne would marry the king's successor were Charles to meet an untimely death — as indeed happened. In her second marriage, Anne became the wife of Louis XII.

The wedding of Anne and Charles took place at the Château de Langeais on December 6th 1491. The future queen spared no expense in order to prove that she was a worthy match for her husband. On this festive occasion, Anne of Brittany, in spite of her lack of funds, displayed great extravagance both in her clothes and her carriages. A detailed description of her travelling outfit reads: 'On this journey Anne wore a lined petticoat made of black satin...the dress worn over this petticoat was of black velvet lined with fine sable; nine yards of velvet and 139 pelts were used in its making. What surpassed everything, however, was the wedding dress itself — gold brocade covered with magnificent appliqué work. This gown was originally lined with fine black lambskins from Lombardy but, because this lining would not look lavish enough, it was replaced by 1160 sable skins.' (Champigneulle.)

The building has remained almost unaltered through the years. Of the original furnishings, on the other hand, hardly anything remains. Nevertheless the rooms appear authentic. Jacques Siegfried who acquired the château 100 years ago is responsible for this. He regarded it as his life's work to restore and furnish it in its original style.

Of special interest are: the fireplace in the *guardroom*, with a mantelpiece in medieval castle style; the *wedding hall* on the first floor with tapestries depicting the 'Nine Valiant Warriors'; other wall hangings from Flanders which make it clear that not only did they have a decorative value but they were also used for insulation; Anne of Brittany's wedding chest; a four-poster bed, one of the first of its kind; and the entwined initials of Anne and Charles which appear everywhere.

The grand *two-storey hall* on the upper floor has a splendid vaulted oak ceiling in the shape of a ship's hull.

The grave of the deserving Monsieur Siegfried, who presented the château to the Institut de France, is in the upper part of the park.

Saumur

Proud and stately, the beautiful Château de Saumur towers over the Loire valley. But its fate is to be constantly compared with a more attractive version of itself in a very famous picture. About the year 1410, the Limbourg brothers produced in the 'Très Riches Heures du duc de Berry' one of the most important works of art of the early Renaissance period. On the page for the month of September is a picture of a castle. Although it looks like a fairytale castle there can be no doubt that fundamentally it is a realistic illustration of the Château de Saumur as it was at that time.

The countryside around Saumur was much fought over by the kings of France and the rulers of Anjou. In 1370, Louis, Duke of Anjou had a new building constructed on the foundations of an older castle. This was to serve a military purpose as well as one of display. The stout walls of the lower part of the building are therefore rather forbidding and without windows, but the higher it gets, the more cheerful its appearance becomes. The Limbourg brothers undoubtedly drew the château in the picture to their own scale. As can be seen today the building is in reality wider; in the picture the vertical aspect dominates, which is explained by the artists' still 'Gothic' way of seeing. Yet we know from many contemporary sources that the roof area of the château was indeed fitted to excess with pinnacles,

turrets, gables, dormers and chimneys. Even the sparkle of the gilded weather vanes has been confirmed.

The festive mood captured in the miniature picture was never experienced at the château. During the Hundred Years War, Saumur often found itself in the centre of battles between the French and English, and in the 16th c. it was repeatedly the focal point in the Religious Wars between the Catholic League and the Huguenots. The governor Duplessis-Mornay, who was appointed by Henri IV, made the château and town more secure with modern fortifications, as it was his intention to turn Saumur into a Protestant stronghold — spiritual as well as material. But history took another course. Following the repeal of the Edict of Nantes in 1685, which had guaranteed freedom of belief to the Protestants, Saumur's importance diminished and the majority of its citizens left the town. The château then began to fall into disrepair and later became a barracks, an arsenal and a jail. It was not until the beginning of the 20th c. that it was acquired by the town, restored and fitted out with two museums.

Immediately you leave the car park, you see the castle from exactly the angle from which it is seen in the picture. You go through a gateway to reach the inner courtyard of the château, where there is a well shaft. You might not wish to visit the dungeon, but do not miss the splendid view over the town, river and the vast hinterland from the top of the *west tower*.

The two museums are worth seeing. In the *Musée des Arts Décoratifs* (Museum of Decorative Art) there are household utensils on display as well as a collection of medieval and Renaissance art, including faience and porcelain, paintings, sculptures in alabaster and wood, wall hangings, furniture and sacred objects. The museum does not overwhelm the visitor with too many items and it is worth admiring selected pieces at leisure, as generally the quality of the exhibits is high.

The *Musée du Cheval* (Museum of the Horse) is regarded as one of the best of its kind in the world. It illustrates the history of the horse's development over 60 million years, from the polydactylous (many-toed) animal the size of a fox to the pedigree English thoroughbred. Everything to do with horseriding and driving has been affectionately collected here: bridles, saddles and harnesses from all parts of the world and from all ages. You will also find detailed information on the history of the *Cadre Noir* which plays such an important role in Saumur (see page 50).

Left: Château de Saumur

Angers

Angers is the ancestral seat of the counts of Anjou, one of the most colourful feudal families in France. Built between 1230 and 1240 on the foundations of a Roman fortress and a Carolingian stronghold, this imposing castle in the shape of a pentagon towers impressively above the valley of the Maine. Charles of Anjou arrived here in 1246. Angers had been made over to him by his brother, Louis IX of France, so that the kingdom would be protected against the ever feared incursions of the Plantagenets.

It was the sinister Charles of Anjou who provoked the 'Sicilian Vespers', a bloody event which took place in 1282. On Easter morning the Sicilians rose up against French foreign rule under Charles, who had been granted the feudal tenure of Sicily by the Pope, and massacred 6000 Frenchmen, most of them from Anjou.

Duke René of Anjou, 'Good King René' (1409–80), was a rather more sympathetic figure. He was one of the most educated people of his time — poet, artist, composer and philosopher — and 'philosophically' allowed Louis XI to claim the duchy of Anjou for the French Crown. Provence also belonged to him and it was there that his life of kindness to his fellow men ended.

At the height of the Religious Wars, Henri III gave orders to raze the entire fortress to the ground so that it would not fall into the hands of the Protestants. It was fortunate that the governor did not carry out these orders immediately, for the king died and it was only the upper storeys of the towers which were demolished.

The château takes the form of an irregular pentagon. It has seventeen round towers which, measured from the bottom of the ditch, are 40–50 m high. Only the tower at the north-west corner has retained its original height and from the platform the view of the town, river and surrounding countryside is quite spectacular. The materials used in the construction of the walls are somewhat unusual: slate alternating with courses of white stone.

You enter the château through the *Porte de Ville*. Gardens are laid out within the walls. The individual buildings — *Logis Royal, Chapelle, Châtelet* and *Logis du Gouverneur* – all date from the 15th c. You can walk along several stretches of the walls.

The most interesting building was actually erected after the Second World War, and its interest lies in what it contains: the *Apocalypse Tapestry Cycle*. The tapestries were commissioned about the year 1370 by Louis, Duke of Anjou. Working from cartoons based on miniatures provided by Hennequin de Bruges, Nicolas Bataille, the most famous weaver of his time, completed the tapestries within five or six years. This was an immense achievement in itself, for there were seven tapestries of 6 m x 24 m, depicting in total ninety-eight scenes from the Apocalypse. Opinions vary as to the original purpose of the tapestries, but it is assumed that they were considered not sufficiently effective in the rooms of the château; King René presented them to the cathedral where they were displayed at festivals.

The later history of the tapestries is somewhat bizarre. By the 18th c. their value was apparently no longer recognised. During the French Revolution they were cut into pieces and used, among other things, as bedcovers. About the middle of the 19th c., however, the bishop of Angers bought back very cheaply what remained of them that was still identifiable. Since then a great deal of

Angers

trouble has been taken to piece together what has been recovered and to trace further fragments. But even now there are still over thirty scenes not accounted for. The importance of the tapestries cannot be overstated, and not only because the cycle is almost certainly the oldest and largest still surviving in Europe. They hold a similar position in the history of tapestry to that of, say, Giotto in painting. What can be seen here, even though it is now only patchwork, will leave a deep impression.

The Apocalypse describes the visions of the apostle John who was exiled on the island of Patmos: visions of the end of the world with all its horrors and suffering, of the rule of the Antichrist and his henchmen, and of his defeat by God in all his glory. The Apocalypse is considered one of the most splendid texts in the New Testament, yet also the most mysterious and obscure. In spite of — or perhaps because of – the richness of the imagery, it is a very difficult task to represent the Apocalypse pictorially. Yet over and over again artists have felt challenged by it to attempt the impossible. Apart from the Angers Apocalypse the most famous such attempt is Dürer's series of woodcuts of 1498. The tapestries are excellently displayed in a room specially built for the purpose. In each case there are explanatory notes opposite the tapestries.

Beauregard

Château de Beauregard

This château has been very aptly named. When the occupants arose each morning they must have been delighted by the beautiful view out over the park to the village of Cellettes and the surrounding countryside.

Of the original château, which was considerably larger in design, only the central wing remains, the appearance of which was altered during the 19th c. by the unsuccessful restoration of the dormer windows. The Italian garden, shown in an etching of about 1550 by Androuet du Cerceau, has been transformed into an English park. The building's original owner was Jean du Thier, who was Henri II's Secretary of State, but who was also known as a humanist and bibliophile. Among all the prominent men in powerful positions, careerists and *nouveaux riches* of his day, he must have been a most agreeable person who — as the position of the château reveals — loved not only books and works of art but also nature.

The main attraction of the château is the *Picture Gallery* on the first floor. It contains 363 portraits of kings, princes, statesmen, soldiers and scholars from the period between Philippe de Valois and Louis XIII. The floor of the gallery is also worth inspecting. It consists entirely of blue and white Delft tiles which depict in twenty-five different motifs an army on the march.

The *Cabinet des Grelots* is also a model of its kind. A small oak-panelled room is decorated in various ways with the heraldic device of the du Thier family (*grelots* are little bells). The still-life paintings which decorate the upper panels are also interesting. Apart from the other beautifully furnished rooms, there is a kitchen equipped as it would have been in the 16th c.

Valençay

Valençay lies a little to the south of the Loire, where Touraine gives place to the former duchy of Berry. Nevertheless, historically and in its appearance it is a genuine Loire château.

Valençay was intended to be the dream castle of an aristocrat, Jacques d'Estampes, who acquired his wealth through marriage. In 1540 work began on a lavishly planned building, but d'Estampes had overstretched himself financially, and only half of this plan was carried out. Work on a more modest scale was resumed at a later date. However, this château with an open view to the south has a proud and elegant air about it.

In 1803 it was discovered by Talleyrand who was then Napoleon's Foreign Minister. Talleyrand had been instructed by the emperor to acquire an imposing château in which high-ranking foreigners and diplomats might be entertained. He therefore proceeded to purchase Valençay, but not before he had demanded and received from Napoleon a considerable proportion of the cost. He then furnished it according to the tastes of the time. The most famous 'guest' was the Spanish king Ferdinand VII, whom Napoleon exiled to Valençay together with his family. While he was living there he was guarded by Talleyrand who had in the meantime fallen into disfavour. Talleyrand survived Napoleon's downfall politically, indeed with spectacular success, but later he displeased Louis XVIII and retired to Valençay.

The *gallery* and some of the *salons* on the ground floor are furnished in the Empire style. Individual items worth inspection include a writing table at which Talleyrand is supposed to have signed the final agreement of the Congress of Vienna, and a portrait by Proudhon of the devious politician. On the upper floor is the *King's Room*, where Ferdinand VII lived during his years of exile here, from 1808 to 1814. Of particular interest are the Italian gouache paintings and the grisaille paintings telling the story of Psyche.

A small museum in a building adjoining the château contains additional Talleyrand memorabilia. In the park in front of the château roam peacocks, herons and storks, while mountain goats climb the steep sides of the former moat. A *Vintage Car Museum* is housed in an outbuilding.

Château de Valençay (MOB-CRTL)

Ussé

The most impressive and elegant view of Ussé is from some distance away, for example on the bridge over the Indre. Set against a background of dark woodland it is an enchanting château, light in character and with countless towers, dormers, pointed turrets and sloping roofs. Surrounding the entire château are projecting battlements. Charles Perrault, the great collector of fairytales, is said to have had Ussé in mind when he wrote his version of 'The Sleeping Beauty'. As you draw nearer to the château the magic diminishes somewhat, and you soon realise that you are faced with a cluster of buildings or parts of buildings on which various periods have left their mark. As with almost every other Loire château, an old fortress once stood on this site; in the second half of the 15th c. work began on the building which survives today. The château was commissioned by the de Bueil family, who sold it in 1485 to Jacques d'Espinay, a vassal of Louis XI. In 1535 work on the building as it was at that time — four wings and an inner courtyard — was completed. The north wing was pulled down in the 17th c. in order to open up the view over the Indre. Other alterations, the last in the 19th c., were carried out in the styles of the periods involved, yet despite this, and although the château has often changed hands, the harmonious overall impression described at the beginning has, remarkably, survived.

 Outside, the guide points out the different architectural features from the various periods. Inside you will be shown an interesting 17th c. Baroque ceiling-painting, a collection of oriental weapons (in the former kitchen) and the *King's Chamber*, set aside for Louis XIV in case he should ever stay here, which in fact never happened. There is a suitably chilly, pompous air about the room — a miniature Versailles.

In the park, a little way from the château, stands the *chapel*, built between 1525 and 1535. It is a typical example of the transitional period between late Gothic and Italian-influenced Renaissance. The chapel is not included in the guided tour, and the architectural details, which are of particular interest, can thus be studied at leisure.

Château d'Ussé

Useful things to know

Before you go

Climate and when to go

Spring (mid-April to mid-June) and autumn (mid-September to mid-October) are generally considered the most pleasant times to visit the Loire Valley. In spring the flow of the river is rapid, the fruit trees are in full blossom, followed by the chestnuts and lilac, and there are few tourists. In the summer the region tends to be crowded and the weather is sometimes oppressive; the water in the Loire is often low and the river is not so attractive. In autumn the light becomes soft and mellow, parks and deciduous forests begin to glow with their changing colours, and streets, car parks and restaurants are not quite as full as in summer. Winter on the Loire is not always cold, but it can be damp.

What to take

Good sunglasses and a suntan lotion are essential. These, together with most items you would normally need on holiday, can be bought locally. However, if you need special glasses or a particular brand of lotion, etc., it is advisable to take these with you.

First-aid kit: You are recommended to take a simple first-aid kit with you. This should include any medicines which have been prescribed or which you regularly use at home, plus remedies for stomach and digestive upsets, headaches and colds, and a supply of pain-killers. For minor injuries pack an elastic bandage, assorted plasters and an antiseptic cream. If your eyes are sensitive to light or strain, include some eye-drops or ointment.

Holiday accommodation

The *Relais et Châteaux* are elegant, rural-style hotels situated within the grounds of châteaux or other stately homes. There are several good ones in the Loire region. The *Logis de France et Auberges rurales* are small to medium-size family hotels in the smaller towns. They give good value for money and are more traditionally French than the larger city hotels. Both groups publish their own hotel guides.

Insurance

You are strongly advised to take out holiday insurance, including cover against medical expenses (unless already covered by private health insurance).

As a member of the EC France has a reciprocal agreement with other EC countries, under which free medical treatment can be obtained for those entitled to it in their own country. To obtain this benefit a UK national has to be in possession of form E111, obtainable from the DSS; an application form is available from the DSS or at main post offices. Anyone travelling by car should be sure to arrange comprehensive insurance cover for the duration of the holiday.

Getting to the Loire Valley

By air: There are direct flights by Air France from Great Britain to Nantes, the only town in this area served by scheduled flights. Alternatively there are internal flights from Paris to Nantes. From the airport cars can be hired to continue the journey (see 'Transport in the area').

By rail: Via Paris there are services to Orléans, Tours, Gien, Nevers, Moulins and Nantes. Many of the places in the Loire Valley can only be reached by road, and rail travellers can make use of the

Train + Auto service organised by French Railways (see 'Transport in the area').

By road: There are frequent cross-Channel car ferry and hovercraft services from the Channel ports to France. From there, via Paris and the A10 motorway, it is about 410 km to Orléans, 535 km to Tours and 695 km to Nantes; on the N7 it is about 550 km to Nevers.

Immigration and Customs

British citizens can enter France with either a full British passport or a British Visitor's Passport.

Customs: Items that can be taken from Great Britain into France and vice versa are the usual EC allowances. If all goods are purchased in shops in an EC country: 8 litres of still table wine, or 5 litres of still table wine plus 1½ litres of spirits or strong liqueurs; 300 cigarettes or tobacco equivalent. If goods are purchased in a duty-free shop on a ship or an aircraft: 4 litres of still table wine or 1 litre of spirits plus 2 litres of still table wine; 200 cigarettes or tobacco equivalent.

During your stay
Chemists and medical help

Chemists' shops have a sign bearing a large green cross. The chemist will be able to give you the address of the nearest doctor or dentist on call and also the addresses of hospitals with casualty departments.

Currency

The unit of currency in France is the franc (F), equal in value to 100 centimes (c). There are coins of 1, 2, 5 and 10 francs and 5, 10, 20 and 50 centimes. There are banknotes for 20, 50, 100 and 500 francs. The exchange rate may be ascertained via banks and the national press. There are no restrictions on the import of foreign currency into France. Eurocheques and travellers' cheques can be cashed in all French banks. The major credit cards are widely accepted in hotels, restaurants and stores, and in many cases can be used to obtain currency from banks.

Electricity

220 volts is now standard virtually throughout France. British plugs do not fit French sockets, and a Continental adaptor is therefore needed before an appliance can be used.

Festivals

May 7th and 8th in Orléans: Jeanne d'Arc Festival with the presentation of colours, bands, military parade, torchlight procession and illuminations.

Mid-June to mid-July in Angers: Anjou Festival with theatre performances and concerts, dance displays, art exhibitions and poetry readings.

Mid-June to mid-July in Sully-sur-Loire: summer concerts.

Last weekend in June and first weekend in July in Grange de Meslay: the Touraine Music Festival held in a monastery barn famous for its good acoustics; initiated by Sviatoslav Richter.

July and August (Saturdays) in Cheverny: hunting-horn concerts.

End of July in Saumur: displays by the *Cadre Noir* from the riding school steeped in tradition.

Opening times

Banks: Generally open 9 a.m.–12 noon and 2–4 p.m., Monday to Friday. Closed at weekends. Some banks close on Mondays.

Châteaux: See 'Visits to the châteaux'.

Churches and monasteries: Usually closed 12 noon–2 p.m.

Government offices: Call between 9 a.m. and 12 noon when they are most likely to be open.

Museums: Large state-owned museums are open on Sundays when admission is free. Privately owned museums are generally closed on Sundays and public holidays. The traditional closing-day for museums is Tuesday but for practical reasons some close on Mondays instead.

Post offices: see 'Post'.

Shops: Larger shops in towns are open 9 a.m.–6.30 p.m. on weekdays. Smaller shops generally close for two hours at midday. Many grocery stores open on Sunday mornings as well, although most are closed on Monday mornings.

Post

Stamps may be purchased at the tobacco kiosks in bars and bistros, and in hotels. Post offices are open Mondays to Fridays 8 a.m. to noon and 2–6 p.m., and Saturdays from 8 a.m. to noon.

Public holidays

January 1st, Easter Monday, May 1st (Labour Day), May 8th (VE Day), Ascension Day, Whit Monday, July 14th (Bastille Day), August 15th (Assumption), November 1st (All Saints' Day), November 11th (Armistice Day), and December 25th.

Son et lumière

These sound and light shows take place after dark during the summer months at the following Loire châteaux: Amboise, Azay-le-Rideau, Blois, Chambord, Chenonceau, Chinon, Loches and Valençay. Episodes of historical interest are presented with dramatic lighting effects which sometimes include the adjoining gardens or park. Dates and times may be obtained from tourist offices.

Telephone

Public telephones are identified by a black and yellow disc-shaped sign. They are sometimes found in bars where they are for public use whether or not you are having a drink. Small plastic phonecards, *télécartes*, obtainable from post offices and *tabacs*, are widely used. When making a call abroad, first dial the international service number (19) and wait for the tone before dialling the code (44 for the UK). International calls are comparatively cheap, although surcharges are imposed by the hotels.

Time

During the winter months France observes Central European Time, one hour ahead of Greenwich Mean Time; Summer Time (GMT + 2 hours) is in force from April to September.

Tipping

A service charge is usually included in hotel and restaurant bills. S.C. = *service compris*. That does not prevent you, however, from giving a tip in recognition of good service. Taxi drivers, porters and hairdressers expect a tip of approximately 8–10% of the bill. Attendants who show people to their seats in the theatre or cinema expect 1–2 francs.

Traffic regulations

Speed limits: In built-up areas 60 km p.h. (37 m.p.h.); outside built-up areas 90 km p.h. (56 m.p.h.), but 80 km p.h. (50 m.p.h.) in rain; on dual carriageways and toll-free urban motorways 110 km p.h. (68 m.p.h.), but 100 km p.h. (62 m.p.h.) in rain; on toll motorways 130 km p.h. (81 m.p.h.), 110 km p.h. (68 m.p.h.) in rain. Drivers who have held a licence for less than one year: 90 km p.h. (56 m.p.h.). Seat belts must be worn at all times. Vehicles travel on the right.

Documents: Driving licence and vehicle registration document must be carried; it is advisable to have a 'Green Card' certificate of insurance.

Filling stations in country areas are sometimes few and far between, or so modestly equipped that it is easy to miss them. Many are closed at lunch-time. Stations selling lead-free petrol (*essence sans plomb*) can be found in most towns and on motorways.

Roads: Even secondary roads in France are well marked out and maintained. Generally speaking they carry little traffic and are a pleasure to use. The 1:250,000 RAC regional maps of France (produced in conjunction with Recta Foldex) are highly recommended, particularly for anyone who enjoys driving on scenic minor roads.

Transport in the area
A journey in the Loire Valley is really only practicable by car for most visitors. The major car-hire firms are represented in the principal towns in the region and at Nantes airport. Travellers by rail can use the Train + Auto scheme whereby arrangements will be made for a hired car to be waiting for them at one of a number of stations in the region.

Another pleasant way of exploring the area is by cycle. Bicycles can be hired from private firms in many towns and, for rail travellers, from stations in the area under the Train + Vélo scheme.

Details of both the above schemes can be obtained from French Railways (see 'Important addresses').

Visits to the châteaux

Opening times: The majority of the châteaux are open during the summer (April 1st to September 30th) 9 a.m.–12 noon and 2–6 or 7 p.m.; in winter 10 a.m.–12 noon and 2–5 p.m.

Guided Tours: In only a few châteaux can visitors look around unaccompanied. Usually a guided tour must be joined and at busy times this may mean a considerable wait.

Entry Fees: Between 8 and 20 francs. Guides usually expect a small gratuity.

Important addresses

British Embassy
35 rue du Faubourg St-Honoré
F-75008 Paris; tel. 1 42 66 91 42

Tourist information offices

French National Tourist Office
178 Piccadilly
London W1V 0AL; tel. (071) 499 6911

On-the-spot information is provided by the *Office de Tourisme* or *Syndicat d'Initiative* in the individual towns.

National motoring organisations

Automobile Club de France, FIA
6–8 Place de la Concorde
F-75008 Paris; tel. 1 42 65 34 70

Association Française des Automobilistes (AFA), FIA & AIT
9 rue Anatole de la Forge
F-75017 Paris; tel. 1 42 27 82 00

French Railways
179 Piccadilly
London W1V 0BA; tel. (071) 493 4451

Useful words and phrases

Although English is often understood in the parts of France frequented by tourists, the visitor will undoubtedly find a few words and phrases of French very useful.

please	s'il vous plaît	ladies	dames
thank you (very much)	merci (bien)	gentlemen	messieurs
		engaged	occupé
yes / no	oui / non	free	libre
excuse me	pardon	entrance	l'entrée
do you speak English?	parlez-vous anglais?	exit	la sortie
I do not understand	je ne comprends pas	today/tomorrow	aujourd'hui/demain
good morning	bonjour	Sunday/Monday	dimanche/lundi
good evening	bonsoir	Tuesday/Wednesday	mardi/mercredi
good night	bonne nuit	Thursday/Friday	jeudi/vendredi
goodbye	au revoir	Saturday/holiday	samedi/jour de congé
how much?	combien?		
I should like	je voudrais	0 zéro	8 huit
a room with private bath	une chambre avec bain	1 un/une	9 neuf
the bill, please!	la note, s'il vous plaît	2 deux	10 dix
(in hotel)		3 trois	11 onze
(in restaurant)	l'addition	4 quatre	12 douze
everything included	tout compris	5 cinq	20 vingt
when?	à quelle heure?	6 six	50 cinquante
open	ouvert	7 sept	100 cent
shut	fermé		
where is ..... street?	où se trouve la rue ......?		

Sully

the road to...?	la route de...?
how far is it to...?	quelle est la distance à...?
to the left / right	à gauche / à droite
straight on	tout droit
post office	le bureau de poste
railway station	la gare
town hall	l'hôtel de ville / la mairie
exchange office	le bureau de change
police station	le commissariat / le poste de police
public telephone	la cabine téléphonique
tourist information office	l'office de tourisme / le syndicat d'initiative
doctor	le médecin
chemist	le pharmacien
toilet	la toilette

Index